The North American Fourth Edition

Cambridge Latin Course

Unit 1

REVISION TEAM

Stephanie Pope, Chair
Norfolk Academy, Norfolk, Virginia

Patricia E. Bell
Centennial Collegiate and Vocational Institute, Guelph, Ontario

Stan Farrow
formerly of the David and Mary Thomson Collegiate Institute, Scarborough, Ontario

Anne Shaw
Lawrence High School and Lawrence Free State High School, Lawrence, Kansas

Randy Thompson
Churchill High School, San Antonio, Texas

CAMBRIDGE
UNIVERSITY PRESS

CAMBRIDGE
UNIVERSITY PRESS

32 Avenue of the Americas, New York, NY 10013–2473, USA

Cambridge University Press is part of the University of Cambridge.

It furthers the University's mission by disseminating knowledge in the pursuit of education, learning and research at the highest international levels of excellence.

www.cambridge.org
Information on this title: www.cambridge.org/9780521004343

The *Cambridge Latin Course* is an outcome of work jointly commissioned by the Schools Council before its closure and the Cambridge School Classics Project, and is published under the aegis of the University of Cambridge School Classics Project and the North American Cambridge Classics Project.

First published 1970
Second edition 1982
Third edition 1988
Fourth edition 2001
24th printing 2014

Printed in the United States of America

Library of Congress Cataloging in Publication Data
Cambridge Latin Course. Unit 1 / revision team, Stephanie Pope ... [et al.].–North American 4th ed.
    p.cm.
    Includes index.
    ISBN 978-0-521-00434-3 (pbk.) – ISBN 978-0-521-78228-9 (hbk.)
    I. Latin Language–Grammar. 2. Latin language–Readers. I. Pope, Stephanie.
  PA 2087.5.C33 2000
478.82'421–dc21   00-037890

ISBN 978-0-521-78228-9 hardback
ISBN 978-0-521-00434-3 paperback

Layout by Newton Harris Design Partnership
Cover photographs by Roger Dalladay
Maps and plans by Robert Calow / Eikon
Illustrations by Peter Kesteven, Neil Sutton, Joy Mellor, and Leslie Jones

Contents

IN MEMORIAM

Ed Phinney

1935–1996

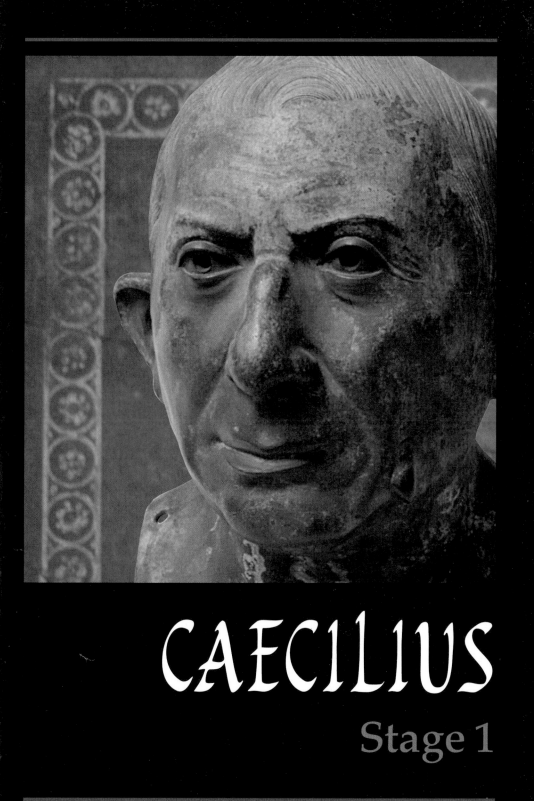

CAECILIUS

Stage 1

familia

1 Caecilius est pater.

2 Metella est māter.

3 Quīntus est fīlius.

4 Clēmēns est servus.

5 Grumiō est coquus.

6 Cerberus est canis.

7 Caecilius est in
tablīnō.

8 Metella est in ātriō.

9 Quīntus est in triclīniō.

10 Clēmēns est in hortō.

11 Grumiō est in culīnā.

12 Cerberus est in viā.

13 pater est in tablīnō.
   pater in tablīnō scrībit.

14 māter est in ātriō.
   māter in ātriō sedet.

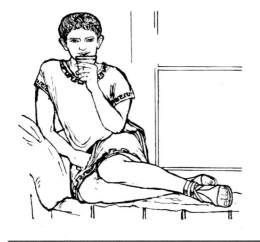

15 fīlius est in triclīniō.
   fīlius in triclīniō bibit.

16 servus est in hortō.
servus in hortō labōrat.

17 coquus est in culīnā.
coquus in culīnā labōrat.

18 canis est in viā.
canis in viā dormit.

est	*is*	in triclīniō	*in the dining room*
pater	*father*	in hortō	*in the garden*
māter	*mother*	in culīnā	*in the kitchen*
fīlius	*son*	in viā	*in the street*
servus	*slave*	scrībit	*is writing*
coquus	*cook*	sedet	*is sitting*
canis	*dog*	bibit	*is drinking*
in tablīnō	*in the study*	labōrat	*is working*
in ātriō	*in the atrium*	dormit	*is sleeping*
	(reception hall)		

Cerberus

Caecilius est in hortō. Caecilius in hortō sedet. servus est in ātriō. servus in ātriō labōrat. Metella est in ātriō. Metella in ātriō sedet. Quīntus est in tablīnō. Quīntus in tablīnō scrībit. Cerberus est in viā.

coquus est in culīnā. coquus in culīnā dormit. Cerberus intrat.   5
Cerberus circumspectat. cibus est in mēnsā. canis salit. canis in mēnsā stat. Grumiō stertit. canis lātrat. Grumiō surgit. coquus est īrātus. "pestis! furcifer!" coquus clāmat. Cerberus exit.

Caecilius had this mosaic of a dog in the doorway of his house.

intrat	*enters*	lātrat	*barks*
circumspectat	*looks around*	surgit	*gets up*
cibus	*food*	īrātus	*angry*
in mēnsā	*on the table*	pestis!	*pest!*
salit	*jumps*	furcifer!	*scoundrel!*
stat	*stands*	clāmat	*shouts*
stertit	*snores*	exit	*goes out*

About the Language

A Latin sentences containing the word **est** often have the same order as English. For example:

Metella est māter.
Metella is the mother.

canis est in viā.
The dog is in the street.

B In other Latin sentences, the order is usually different from that of English. For example:

canis in viā dormit.
The dog is sleeping in the street.

servus in culīnā labōrat.
The slave is working in the kitchen.

C Note that **dormit** and **labōrat** in the sentences above can be translated in another way. For example: **servus in culīnā labōrat** can mean *The slave works in the kitchen* as well as *The slave is working in the kitchen*. The story will help you to decide which translation gives the better sense.

Reconstruction of a Roman kitchen.

Practicing the Language

Write out each Latin sentence, completing it with a suitable word or phrase from the box. Then translate the sentence. Use each word or phrase only once.

For example: ..... est in hortō.
servus est in hortō.
The slave is in the garden.

A 1 ..... est in hortō.
  2 ..... est in viā.
  3 ..... est in culīnā.
  4 ..... est in tablīnō.
  5 ..... est in ātriō.
  6 ..... est in triclīniō.

Quīntus	canis
Grumiō	māter
Caecilius	servus

B 1 Clēmēns ..... labōrat.
  2 Caecilius ..... scrībit.
  3 canis ..... lātrat.
  4 Metella ..... stat.
  5 coquus est ......
  6 Quīntus est ......

in viā	in tablīnō
in hortō	in culīnā
in ātriō	in triclīniō

Detail from a wall-painting from a villa near Pompeii.

Caecilius

Caecilius lived in Italy during the first century A.D. in the town of Pompeii. The town was situated at the foot of Mount Vesuvius on the coast of the Bay of Naples and may have had a population of about 10,000. Caecilius was a rich Pompeian banker. When archaeologists excavated his house, they discovered his accounts in a strongbox; these documents tell us that he was also an auctioneer, tax collector, farmer, and moneylender.

He inherited some of his money from his father, Lucius Caecilius Felix, but he probably made most of it through shrewd and energetic business activities. He dealt in slaves, cloth, timber, and property. He also ran a cleaning and dyeing business, grazed sheep and cattle on pastures outside the town, and sometimes won the contract for collecting the local taxes. He may have owned a few shops as well and probably lent money to local shipping companies wishing to trade with countries overseas. The profit on such trading was often very large.

Caecilius' full name was Lucius Caecilius Iucundus. Lucius was his personal name, rather like a modern first name. His second name, Caecilius, shows that he was a member of the "clan" of the Caecilii. Clans or groups of families were very important and strong feelings of loyalty existed within them. Caecilius' third name, Iucundus, is the name of his own family and close relatives. The word **Iucundus** means "pleasant," just as in English we find surnames like Pleasance or Jolly.

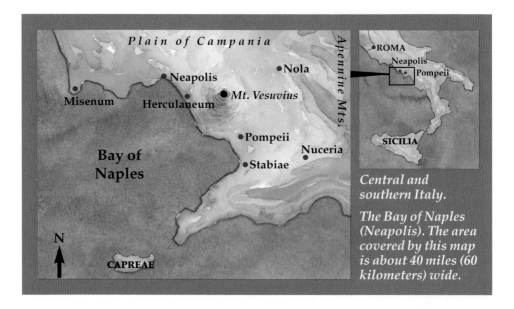

Central and southern Italy.

The Bay of Naples (Neapolis). The area covered by this map is about 40 miles (60 kilometers) wide.

Only a Roman citizen would have three names. A slave would have just one, such as Clemens or Grumio. As a Roman citizen, Caecilius not only had the right to vote in elections but also was fully protected by the law against unjust treatment. The slaves who lived and worked in his house and in his businesses had no rights of their own. They were his property, and he could treat them as well or as badly as he wished. There was one important exception to this rule: the law did not allow a master to put a slave to death without showing good reason.

The front of Caecilius' house. The spaces on either side of the door were shops that he probably owned.

This head found in Caecilius' house may be a portrait of him.

This is one of the wooden tablets found in Caecilius' house. They recorded his business dealings. The writing was on wax in the central recess, and, when the tablets were discovered, much of the writing could still be read. The tablets were tied together in twos or threes through the holes at the top.

Caecilius kept his tablets and money in a wood and metal strongbox like this.

One page of writing: it records the sale at auction of a slave for 6,252 sesterces.

Metella

Roman women of all classes had much greater personal freedom than women in other parts of the Mediterranean. Caecilius' wife, Metella, like many Roman wives and mothers, had an important position in her home. She was responsible for the efficient and economical management of the household. She supervised the work of the domestic slaves. In order to run the house successfully, she would need to be well organized and firm but sensitive in her control of the slaves.

Although complete equality of the sexes was never an issue in ancient Rome, the Roman wife often had considerable power, influence, and freedom of behavior. She enjoyed her husband's confidence; she was his companion and helper; she shared his authority over the children and slaves; she shared responsibility for the religious cult of the family; she prepared for social occasions and helped to welcome guests; she dined next to her husband at banquets (a practice Greeks would have condemned as disgraceful); she played a part in his career if it took him on a tour of duty to the provinces.

Unlike women in Greece or the Near East, Roman women were not required to live in seclusion in the home. Although their lives did center on the home, Roman women of all classes went out to shop, to exchange visits with friends, to go to the baths, to worship at temples, to attend public events in the theater or amphitheater, and to accompany their husbands to banquets where they took a well-informed part in social and literary conversation. We know of women who were cooks, bakers, weavers, hairdressers, shoemakers, silversmiths, midwives, and doctors. Occasionally women engaged in business. Often such women were widows who took over control of their husbands' affairs. One influential Pompeian businesswoman was Eumachia (*right*), a public priestess and patroness of the powerful clothworkers and merchants. She inherited money from her father, who had owned a brickmaking business. It was her donation of money that built the large meeting hall of the cloth trade in Pompeii.

Eumachia, a Pompeian businesswoman who built the Clothworkers' Meeting Hall in the forum.

Houses in Pompeii

The town house in which a wealthy man like Caecilius lived differed in several ways from an equivalent house today. The house came right up to the sidewalk; there was no garden or grass in front of it. The windows were few, small, and placed fairly high. They were intended to let in light but to keep out the heat of the sun. Large windows would have made the rooms uncomfortably hot in summer and cold in winter.

Some houses stood only one story high; others had a second floor. On either side of the front door, many houses had shops, which were rented out by the owner of the house. From the outside, with its few windows and high walls, the house did not look very attractive or inviting.

The ground plan of the house shows two parts or areas of about equal size. They look like courtyards surrounded by rooms opening off the central space.

The main entrance to the house was on the side facing the street. On passing through the door, the **iānua**, the visitor came into a short corridor which led directly into the main room, the **ātrium**. This impressive room was used for important family occasions and for receiving visitors. In the middle, the roof sloped down slightly towards a large square opening called the **compluvium**. Air and light streamed in through this opening, high overhead. Immediately below was the **impluvium**, a marble-lined, shallow rectangular pool that collected rainwater, which was then stored in a cistern for household use.

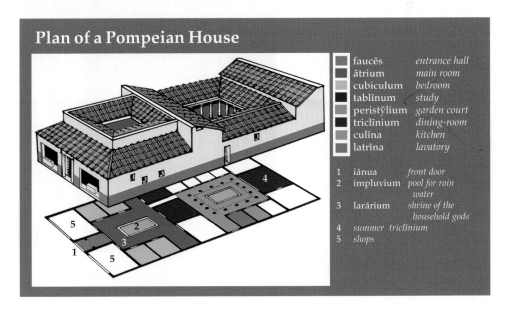

Plan of a Pompeian House

faucēs	entrance hall
ātrium	main room
cubiculum	bedroom
tablīnum	study
peristȳlium	garden court
triclīnium	dining-room
culīna	kitchen
latrīna	lavatory

1	iānua	front door
2	impluvium	pool for rain water
3	larārium	shrine of the household gods
4		summer triclīnium
5		shops

One of the most striking things about the atrium was the sense of space. The high roof with the glimpse of the sky through the central opening, the large floor area, and the absence of much furnishing all helped to give this impression. The furniture would include a bronze or marble table, a couch, and perhaps a strongbox in which the family valuables were stored. In a corner, near the main door, there was the **larārium**, a small shrine at which the family gods were worshipped. The floor of the atrium was paved with marble slabs or with mosaics. The walls were decorated with panels of brightly painted plaster. The Pompeians were especially fond of red, orange, and blue. On many of these panels there were scenes from well-known stories, especially the Greek myths.

Around the atrium were arranged the bedrooms, the study, and the dining room. The entrances to these rooms were usually provided not with a wooden door but with a heavy curtain.

*Below: **The atrium in Caecilius' house as it is today. We can see how spacious it was, but for a real sense of the dignity of an atrium, we need to look at a better preserved one** (right)**. The visitor entering the front door would see, beyond the impluvium, the tablinum and the sunlit peristylium.***

From this first area of the house, the visitor walked either through the **tablīnum** (study) or through a narrow passage into the second part. This was the **peristȳlium**, which was made up of a colonnade of pillars surrounding the **hortus** (garden). Like the atrium, the colonnade was often elaborately decorated. Around the outside of the colonnade were the summer dining room, the kitchen, the toilet, slaves' quarters, and storage rooms. Some houses even had their own set of baths.

The garden was laid out with flowers and shrubs in a careful plan. In the small fishpond in the middle, a fountain threw up a jet of water. Marble statues of gods and heroes stood here and there. In the peristylium, the members of the family enjoyed the sunshine or shade as they wished; here they relaxed on their own or entertained their guests.

The Pompeians not only lived in houses that looked very different from modern ones but also thought very differently about them. They did not expect their houses to be private places restricted to the family and close friends. Instead, the master conducted much of his business and social life from home. He would receive and do business with most visitors in the atrium. The more important ones would be invited into the tablinum. Certain very close business friends and high-ranking individuals would receive invitations to dine in the **triclīnium** or relax in the peristylium with the family.

Only the wealthy lived like this; poor people lived in much simpler homes. Some of the poorer shopkeepers would have had only a room or two above their shops. In large cities, such as Rome, many people lived in **īnsulae**, apartment buildings several stories high, some of them in very poor condition.

A peristylium with hanging ornaments between the columns.

In what ways is this house typical of houses in Caecilius' day?

A painting of a marble fountain in a garden.

Three-legged table in the tablinum of the House of Paquius Proculus.

A lararium.

Word Study

A In the Stage 1 Vocabulary Checklist, find the Latin word from which these words are derived:

1 serf
2 patrician
3 elaborate
4 concoct
5 culinary
6 matrimony
7 collaborate
8 deviate

B Match each definition with one of the words given below:

affiliate   laboratory   sedentary
canine   maternity   service
horticulturalist

1 . . . . .   a room or building used for scientific testing or research
2 . . . . .   a person who works with plants
3 . . . . .   motherhood
4 . . . . .   the act of providing goods or assistance
5 . . . . .   pertaining to dogs
6 . . . . .   tending to be inactive
7 . . . . .   to associate or join oneself

While the butcher cuts meat, his wife may be working on the accounts.

Stage 1
Vocabulary Checklist

ātrium	atrium, reception hall
canis	dog
coquus	cook
cubiculum	bedroom
culīna	kitchen
est	is
fīlius	son
hortus	garden
in	in, on
labōrat	works, is working
māter	mother
pater	father
sedet	sits, is sitting
servus	slave
tablīnum	study
triclīnium	dining room
via	street

Metella was very fond of jewelry. Here are some examples of the things she might have worn.

IN VILLA

amīcus

1 Caecilius est in ātriō.

2 amīcus Caecilium salūtat.

3 Metella est in ātriō.

4 amīcus Metellam salūtat.

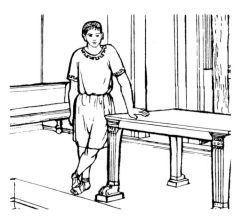

5 Quīntus est in ātriō.

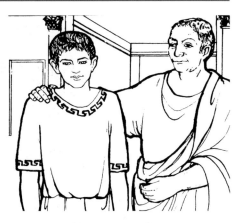

6 amīcus Quīntum salūtat.

7 servus est in ātriō.

8 amīcus servum salūtat.

9 canis est in ātriō.

10 amīcus canem salūtat.

Metella

11 coquus est in culīnā.

12 Metella culīnam intrat.

13 Grumiō labōrat.

14 Metella Grumiōnem spectat.

15 cibus est parātus.

16 Metella cibum gustat.

17 Grumiō est anxius.

18 Metella Grumiōnem laudat.

19 amīcus est in hortō.

20 Metella amīcum vocat.

mercātor

amīcus Caecilium vīsitat. amīcus est mercātor. mercātor vīllam intrat. Clēmēns est in ātriō. Clēmēns mercātōrem salūtat. Caecilius est in tablīnō. Caecilius pecūniam numerat. Caecilius est argentārius. amīcus tablīnum intrat. Caecilius surgit.

"salvē!" Caecilius mercātōrem salūtat. 5

"salvē!" mercātor respondet.

Caecilius triclīnium intrat. amīcus quoque intrat. amīcus in lectō recumbit. argentārius in lectō recumbit.

Grumiō in culīnā cantat. Grumiō pāvōnem coquit. coquus est laetus. Caecilius coquum audit. Caecilius nōn est laetus. Caecilius 10
cēnam exspectat. amīcus cēnam exspectat. Caecilius Grumiōnem vituperat.

mercātor	merchant
amīcus	friend
vīsitat	is visiting
vīllam	house
salūtat	greets
pecūniam	money
numerat	is counting
argentārius	banker
salvē!	hello!
respondet	replies
quoque	also, too
in lectō	on a couch
recumbit	reclines
cantat	is singing
pāvōnem	peacock
coquit	is cooking
laetus	happy
audit	hears, listens to
nōn est	is not
cēnam	dinner
exspectat	is waiting for
vituperat	tells off, curses

in triclīniō

Grumiō triclīnium intrat. Grumiō pāvōnem portat. Clēmēns triclīnium intrat. Clēmēns vīnum portat. Caecilius pāvōnem gustat.

"pāvō est optimus!" Caecilius clāmat.

mercātor quoque pāvōnem gustat. mercātor cēnam laudat. 5 dominus coquum laudat. Grumiō exit.

ancilla intrat. ancilla suāviter cantat. ancilla dominum dēlectat. ancilla mercātōrem dēlectat. mox dominus dormit. amīcus quoque dormit.

Grumiō triclīnium intrat et circumspectat. coquus cibum in 10 mēnsā videt. Grumiō cibum cōnsūmit et vīnum bibit! Caecilius Grumiōnem nōn videt. coquus in triclīniō magnificē cēnat.

coquus ancillam spectat. ancilla Grumiōnem dēlectat. Grumiō ancillam dēlectat. Grumiō est laetissimus.

portat	*is carrying*
vīnum	*wine*
gustat	*tastes*
optimus	*very good, excellent*
laudat	*praises*
dominus	*master*
ancilla	*slave-girl*
suāviter	*sweetly*
dēlectat	*pleases*
mox	*soon*
et	*and*
videt	*sees*
cōnsūmit	*eats*
magnificē	*magnificently, in style*
cēnat	*eats dinner, dines*
spectat	*looks at*
laetissimus	*very happy*

About the Language

A Words like **Metella**, **Caecilius**, and **mercātor** are known as nouns. They often indicate people or animals (e.g. **ancilla**, **canis**), places (e.g. **vīlla**, **hortus**), and things (e.g. **cēna**, **cibus**).

B You have now met two forms of the same noun:

    Metella – Metellam
    Caecilius – Caecilium
    mercātor – mercātōrem

C The different forms are known as the **nominative case** and the **accusative case**.

    nominative Metella   Caecilius   mercātor
    accusative Metellam   Caecilium   mercātōrem

D If Metella does something, such as praising Grumio, the nominative **Metella** is used:

    Metella Grumiōnem laudat.
    Metella praises Grumio.

E But if somebody else does something to Metella, the accusative **Metellam** is used:

    amīcus **Metellam** salūtat.
    The friend greets Metella.

F Notice again the difference in word order between Latin and English:

    coquus culīnam intrat.
    The cook enters the kitchen.

    Clēmēns vīnum portat.
    Clemens carries the wine.

Practicing the Language

A Write out each Latin sentence, completing it with a suitable word or phrase from the box. Then translate the sentence. Use each phrase only once.

> For example: canis . . . . . stat.
> canis **in viā** stat.
> *The dog is standing in the street.*

1 Grumiō . . . . . coquit.
2 . . . . . in hortō labōrat.
3 mercātor in tablīnō . . . . . .
4 Cerberus . . . . . dormit.
5 Metella in ātriō . . . . . .
6 . . . . . in triclīniō cēnat.

scrībit	amīcus
in culīnā	sedet
servus	in viā

B Write out each Latin sentence, completing it with the correct word from the parentheses. Then translate the sentence.

> For example: amīcus Caecilium . . . . . (sedet, vīsitat).
> amīcus Caecilium **vīsitat**.
> *A friend visits Caecilius.*

1 Caecilius pecūniam (numerat, dormit).
2 Clēmēns vīnum (labōrat, portat).
3 ancilla hortum (intrat, gustat).
4 Metella mercātōrem (salūtat, cantat).
5 Quīntus cēnam (vīsitat, cōnsūmit).
6 servus vīllam (dormit, intrat, portat).
7 amīcus Grumiōnem (spectat, stat, recumbit).
8 māter fīlium (surgit, dormit, vituperat).
9 mercātor canem (sedet, cōnsūmit, audit).
10 dominus ancillam (scrībit, laudat, numerat).

C Write out each sentence, choosing the noun that correctly completes the sentence. Translate each sentence.

1 (servus, servum) in culīnā coquit.
2 māter (mercātor, mercātōrem) salūtat.
3 (ancilla, ancillam) suāviter cantat.
4 servus (cēna, cēnam) gustat.
5 Grumiō (ancilla, ancillam) dēlectat.
6 (dominus, dominum) dormit.

D Translate into English:

amīcus

amīcus Grumiōnem vīsitat. amīcus est servus. servus vīllam intrat. Clēmēns est in ātriō. servus Clēmentem videt. Clēmēns servum salūtat. servus culīnam intrat. servus culīnam circumspectat.

Grumiō nōn est in culīnā. servus cibum videt. cibus est 5 parātus! servus cibum gustat. cibus est optimus.

Grumiō culīnam intrat. Grumiō amīcum videt. amīcus cibum cōnsūmit! coquus est īrātus.

"pestis! furcifer!" coquus clāmat. coquus amīcum vituperat. *10*

parātus *ready*

Food excavated at Pompeii: walnuts and olives.

Above: **the garden from the House of the Vettii.** *Below:* **the summer triclinium from a house in Herculaneum.**

Daily Life

The day began early for Caecilius and the members of his household. He would usually get up at dawn. His slaves were up even earlier, sweeping, dusting, and polishing.

It did not take Caecilius long to dress. The first garment that he put on was his **tunica**, a tunic similar to a short-sleeved shirt, then his **toga**, a very large piece of woolen cloth arranged in folds, and finally his shoes, which were rather like modern sandals. A quick wash of the hands and face with cold water was enough at that time of the morning. Later he would visit a barber to be shaved, and in the afternoon he would enjoy a leisurely visit to the public baths.

His wife, Metella, also got up early. Over her tunica, she put on a **stola**, a full-length over-tunic. If she were going out, she would also wear a large rectangular shawl, called a **palla**. With the help of a skilled slave-woman, she did her hair in the latest style, put on her makeup, including powder, rouge, and mascara, and chose her jewelry from her large and varied collection.

Breakfast was only a light snack, often just a cup of water and a piece of bread. The first duty of the day for Caecilius was to receive the respectful greetings of a number of poorer people and freedmen who had previously been his slaves. The **salūtātiō** or reception of these visitors took place in the atrium. Caecilius would hand out small sums of money to them. If they were in any kind of trouble, he gave them as much help and protection as he could. In return, they helped Caecilius in several ways. They might accompany him to show support on public occasions, and they might also be employed by him in business affairs. They were known as his **clientēs** (clients), and he was their **patrōnus** (patron). If, after seeing these visitors, he had no further business to conduct at home, Caecilius set out for the **forum** (market-place), where he spent the rest of the morning trading and banking.

An important Roman dressed in his toga. This hot and unwieldy garment was valued because only citizens could wear it.

Lunch was eaten at about midday, and it was also a light meal. It usually consisted of some meat or fish followed by fruit. Business ended soon after lunch. Caecilius would then have a short siesta before going to the baths. Towards the end of the afternoon, the main meal of the day began. This was called the **cēna**.

During the winter, the family used the inner dining room near the atrium. In the summer, they would generally have preferred the dining room at the back of the house, which looked straight out onto the garden. Three couches were arranged around a **mēnsa** or circular table which, though small, was very elegantly carved and decorated. Each couch had places for three people. The

Bankers in the forum.

diners reclined on the couches, leaning on their left elbow and taking food from the table with their right hand. The food was cut up by a slave before being served, and diners ate it with their fingers or a spoon. Forks were not used by the Romans.

By the time of our stories, the women of the family were present at the cena, usually reclining like the men. The meal was not hurried, for this was an occasion to talk and relax over good food. Women played an active role in the conversation, even on social occasions. If guests were invited, some form of entertainment was often provided.

Not all Romans reclined when eating dinner, but it was usual among rich or upper-class families. Poor people, slaves, children, and sometimes women would eat sitting up.

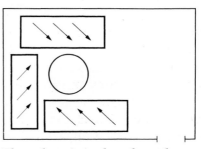

These drawings show how the couches were arranged in a Roman dining room. The Latin name "triclinium" means a room with three couches.

A Roman Dinner

The meal began with a first course of light dishes to whet the appetite. Eggs, fish, and cooked and raw vegetables were often served. Then came the main course in which a variety of meat dishes with different sauces and vegetables would be offered. Beef, pork, mutton, and poultry were all popular, and in preparing them the cook would do his best to show off his skill and imagination. Finally, the dessert was brought in, consisting of fruit, nuts, cheese, and sweet dishes. During the meal, wine produced locally from the vineyards on Mount Vesuvius was served, usually mixed with water. Women were expected to drink sparingly.

Roman dinners were said to run ab ovo usque ad mala ("from eggs to apples"); this bowl of eggs has survived from Pompeii.

Fish and other seafood were much enjoyed.

Many loaves of bread have been found in the ruins of Pompeii.

Main course ingredients – a rabbit and a chicken – hanging in a larder.

To round off the meal: the fruit bowl and the basket of figs.

Word Study

A Give the Latin word in the Stage 2 Vocabulary Checklist from which the following words are derived. Select the definition for each derivative.

1 amicable		**a**	trade
2 ancillary		**b**	friendly
3 gustatory		**c**	overpowering or controlling
4 domineering		**d**	pertaining to taste
5 dormant		**e**	expressing praise
6 laudatory		**f**	a military greeting
7 salute		**g**	inactive, as if asleep
8 commerce		**h**	helpful

B Give a derivative from the Stage 2 Vocabulary Checklist to match each definition:

1 likeable
2 formal greeting
3 the area over which one rules
4 worthy of praise
5 sleeping quarters
6 strong distaste
7 a mountain with a top as flat as a table

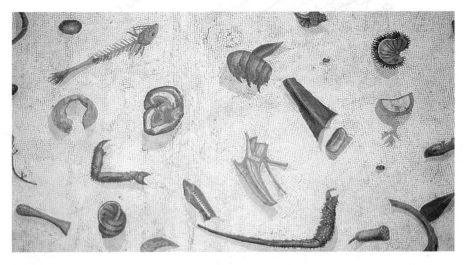

Part of a mosaic floor, showing the scraps left behind by the diners after a cena.

Stage 2
Vocabulary Checklist

amīcus	*friend*
ancilla	*slave-girl, slave-woman*
cēna	*dinner*
cibus	*food*
dominus	*master*
dormit	*sleeps*
gustat	*tastes*
intrat	*enters*
laetus	*happy*
laudat	*praises*
mēnsa	*table*
mercātor	*merchant*
quoque	*also, too*
salūtat	*greets*
toga	*toga*
tunica	*tunic*

Grumio did most of his cooking with pans and grills over charcoal, like a barbecue.

NEGOTIUM

Stage 3

in forō

Caecilius nōn est in vīllā. Caecilius in forō negōtium agit. Caecilius est argentārius. argentārius pecūniam numerat.

Caecilius forum circumspectat. ecce! pictor in forō ambulat. pictor est Celer. Celer Caecilium salūtat.

ecce! tōnsor quoque est in forō. tōnsor est Pantagathus. 5 Caecilius tōnsōrem videt.

"salvē!" Caecilius tōnsōrem salūtat.

"salvē!" Pantagathus respondet.

ecce! vēnālīcius forum intrat. vēnālīcius est Syphāx. vēnālīcius mercātōrem exspectat. mercātor nōn venit. Syphāx est īrātus. 10 Syphāx mercātōrem vituperat.

in forō	*in the forum*
negōtium agit	*is working, is doing business*
ecce!	*see! look!*
pictor	*painter, artist*
ambulat	*is walking*
tōnsor	*barber*
vēnālīcius	*slave-dealer*
nōn venit	*does not come*

pictor

pictor ad vīllam venit. pictor est Celer. Celer iānuam pulsat.
Clēmēns pictōrem nōn audit. servus est in hortō. Celer clāmat.
canis Celerem audit et lātrat. Quīntus canem audit. Quīntus ad
iānuam venit. fīlius iānuam aperit. Celer Quīntum salūtat et vīllam
intrat. 5

Metella est in culīnā. Quīntus mātrem vocat. Metella ātrium
intrat. pictor Metellam salūtat. Metella pictōrem ad triclīnium
dūcit.

Celer in triclīniō labōrat. Celer pictūram pingit. magnus leō est
in pictūrā. Herculēs quoque est in pictūrā. leō Herculem ferōciter 10
petit. Herculēs magnum fūstem tenet et leōnem verberat. Herculēs
est fortis.

Caecilius ad vīllam revenit et triclīnium intrat. Caecilius
pictūram intentē spectat et pictūram laudat.

ad vīllam	*to the house*	**leō**	*lion*
iānuam	*door*	**ferōciter**	*fiercely*
pulsat	*knocks on/at*	**petit**	*heads for, attacks*
aperit	*opens*	**fūstem**	*club*
vocat	*calls*	**tenet**	*is holding*
dūcit	*leads*	**verberat**	*is striking*
pictūram	*picture*	**fortis**	*brave, strong*
pingit	*paints*	**revenit**	*returns*
magnus	*big, large*	**intentē**	*intently*

*Wall-paintings
from Pompeii.*

tōnsor

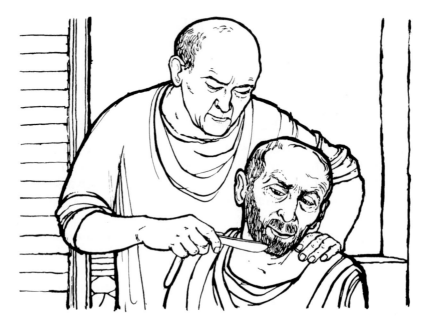

When you have read this story, answer the questions opposite in English unless you are asked for the Latin.

tōnsor in tabernā labōrat. tōnsor est Pantagathus. Caecilius intrat.

   "salvē, tōnsor!" inquit Caecilius.

   "salvē!" respondet Pantagathus.

   tōnsor est occupātus. senex in sellā sedet. Pantagathus novāculam tenet et barbam tondet. senex novāculam intentē   *5* spectat.

   poēta tabernam intrat. poēta in tabernā stat et versum recitat. Caecilius rīdet, sed tōnsor nōn rīdet. versus est scurrīlis; tōnsor est īrātus.

   "furcifer! furcifer!" clāmat Pantagathus. senex est perterritus.   *10* tōnsor barbam nōn tondet. tōnsor senem secat. multus sanguis fluit.

   Caecilius surgit et ē tabernā exit.

in tabernā	*in the shop*
inquit	*says*
occupātus	*busy*
senex	*old man*
in sellā	*in the chair*
novāculam	*razor*
barbam	*beard*
tondet	*is trimming*
poēta	*poet*
versum	*a line, a verse*
recitat	*recites*
rīdet	*laughs, smiles*
sed	*but*
scurrīlis	*obscene, dirty*
perterritus	*terrified*
secat	*cuts*
multus	*much*
sanguis	*blood*
fluit	*flows*
ē tabernā	*out of the shop*

Barber's shears.

Questions

1 Who is working in the shop when Caecilius arrives?
2 **tōnsor est occupātus** (line 4). Look at the rest of the paragraph and say why the barber is described as busy.
3 In line 7, who else comes into the shop?
4 **Caecilius rīdet** (line 8). What makes Caecilius laugh?
5 In lines 8–9, what is the barber's reaction?
6 In line 11, what does the barber do to the old man?
7 What does Caecilius do at the end of the story? Why do you think he does this?
8 Look at the drawing opposite. Which Latin sentence best explains the old man's expression?

vēnālīcius

Caecilius ad portum ambulat. Caecilius portum circumspectat.
argentārius nāvem Syriam videt et ad nāvem ambulat. Syphāx
prope nāvem stat.

"salvē, Syphāx!" clāmat argentārius. Syphāx est vēnālīcius.
Syphāx Caecilium salūtat.   5

Caecilius servum quaerit. Syphāx rīdet. ecce! Syphāx magnum
servum habet. Caecilius servum spectat. argentārius nōn est
contentus. argentārius servum nōn emit.

"vīnum!" clāmat Syphāx. ancilla vīnum bonum ad Caecilium
portat. argentārius vīnum bibit.   10

Caecilius ancillam spectat. ancilla est pulchra. ancilla rīdet.
ancilla Caecilium dēlectat. vēnālīcius quoque rīdet.

"Melissa cēnam optimam coquit," inquit vēnālīcius. "Melissa
linguam Latīnam discit. Melissa est docta et pulchra. Melissa ..."

"satis! satis!" clāmat Caecilius. Caecilius Melissam emit et ad   15
vīllam revenit. Melissa Grumiōnem dēlectat. Melissa Quīntum
dēlectat. ēheu! ancilla Metellam nōn dēlectat.

ad portum	*to the harbor*	bonum	*good*
nāvem Syriam	*Syrian ship*	pulchra	*beautiful*
prope nāvem	*near the ship*	linguam Latīnam	*Latin language*
quaerit	*is searching for,*	discit	*is learning*
	is looking for	docta	*skillful, good at*
habet	*has*		*her job*
contentus	*satisfied*	satis	*enough*
emit	*buys*	ēheu!	*alas! oh dear!*

About the Language

A Remember the difference between the nominative case and accusative case of the following nouns:

nominative	Metella	Caecilius	mercātor
accusative	Metellam	Caecilium	mercātōrem

B A large number of words, such as **ancilla** and **taberna**, form their accusative case in the same way as **Metella**. They belong to a "family" of nouns known as the **first declension** and look like this:

nominative	Metella	ancilla	taberna
accusative	Metellam	ancillam	tabernam

The nominative ending of the first declension is **-a**, and the accusative ends in **-am**.

C Another large group of nouns belongs to the **second declension**. Most of these words form their accusative in the same way as **Caecilius**. For example:

nominative	Caecilius	servus	amīcus
accusative	Caecilium	servum	amīcum

The nominative ending of the second declension is usually **-us**, and the accusative ends in **-um**.

D You have also met several nouns belonging to the **third declension**. For example:

nominative	mercātor	leō	senex	canis
accusative	mercātōrem	leōnem	senem	canem

The nominative ending of the third declension may take various forms, but the accusative nearly always ends in **-em**.

Practicing the Language

A Write out each sentence, completing it with the correct word in parentheses. Then translate the sentence into English.

1 mercātor ē vīllā (quaerit, ambulat).
2 servus ad hortum (recitat, venit).
3 coquus ad culīnam (revenit, habet).
4 Syphāx servum ad vīllam (dūcit, intrat).
5 Clēmēns cibum ad Caecilium (salit, respondet, portat).

B The following words are all in the nominative case:

pictor
Celer
iānua
canis
Quīntus
Metella
pictūra
leō
Herculēs

Find their accusative forms in the story, **pictor**, on page 37. Make three lists of their accusative forms to coincide with their declensions, as explained on page 41.

C Write out each sentence, completing it with the correct case of the noun in parentheses. Then translate the sentence into English.

For example: (servus, servum) vīnum portat.
servus vīnum portat.
The slave carries the wine.

1 amīcus (servus, servum) laudat.
2 senex (taberna, tabernam) intrat.
3 (dominus, dominum) cibum gustat.
4 (mercātor, mercātōrem) Metellam salūtat.
5 vēnālīcius (tōnsor, tōnsōrem) videt.
6 (poēta, poētam) versum recitat.
7 (senex, senem) in forō ambulat.
8 ancilla (pictor, pictōrem) ad ātrium dūcit.

The Town of Pompeii

Intersection of two streets in Pompeii. The house has its second floor overhanging the road to gain a little extra floor space.

The town of Pompeii was built on a low hill of volcanic rock about five miles (eight kilometers) south of Mount Vesuvius and close to the mouth of a small river. It was one of a number of prosperous towns in the fertile region of Campania. Outside the towns, especially along the coast of the bay, there were many villas and farming estates, often owned by wealthy Romans who were attracted to the area by its pleasant climate and peaceful surroundings.

Villas along the bay.

The town itself covered 163 acres (66 hectares) and was surrounded by a wall. The wall had eleven towers and eight gates. Roads led out from these gates to the neighboring towns of Herculaneum, Nola, Nuceria, and Stabiae, and to the harbor.

Two wide main streets, known today as the Street of Shops and Stabiae Street, crossed near the center of the town. A third main street ran parallel to the Street of Shops. The other streets, most of which also ran in straight lines, divided the town neatly into blocks. Most streets probably did not have names, and a stranger visiting the town would have had to ask the way from the local people. The present names were invented in modern times to make identification and location of buildings easier. The streets, constructed of volcanic stone, had high paved sidewalks on one or both sides to enable pedestrians to avoid the traffic of wagons, horses, and mules and to keep out of the garbage and rainwater that collected in the roadway. Stepping stones provided convenient crossing places.

A street in Pompeii in the rain.

Stabiae Street today.

In all the main streets there were bakers' shops and bars where hot and cold drinks and snacks could be bought. The main shopping areas were in the forum and along the Street of Shops to the northeast of the Stabian baths. Carved or painted signs indicated different kinds of stores: the figure of a goat announced a dairy; a hammer and chisel advertised a stonemason. General advertisements and public notices were painted on the whitewashed walls outside shops and houses. We can still see notices advertising shows in the amphitheater and political slogans supporting candidates in the local elections.

A bakery. On the left are three grain mills, worked by slaves or donkeys, and at the back is the bread oven.

At the western end of the town was the **forum**. This large and impressive open space, with a covered colonnade on three sides, was the center for business, local government, and religion.

There were two theaters. Popular shows for large audiences were performed in the big open-air theater, which could hold about 5,000 people, while the smaller one, which was roofed, was used for concerts and for other shows. At the eastern end of the town was a huge sports ground and next to it an amphitheater in which gladiatorial combats and wild animal hunts were staged. This amphitheater was large enough to seat every inhabitant in Pompeii and visitors from neighboring towns as well.

Like a modern seaport, Pompeii was a place where people of many nationalities were to be seen: Romans, Greeks, Syrians, Jews, Africans, Spaniards, and probably several other nationalities as well, with their different languages and different religions. This regular coming and going of people, many of whom were merchants and businessmen, was made possible by the peaceful conditions that existed throughout the provinces of the Roman Empire at this time.

Pompeii

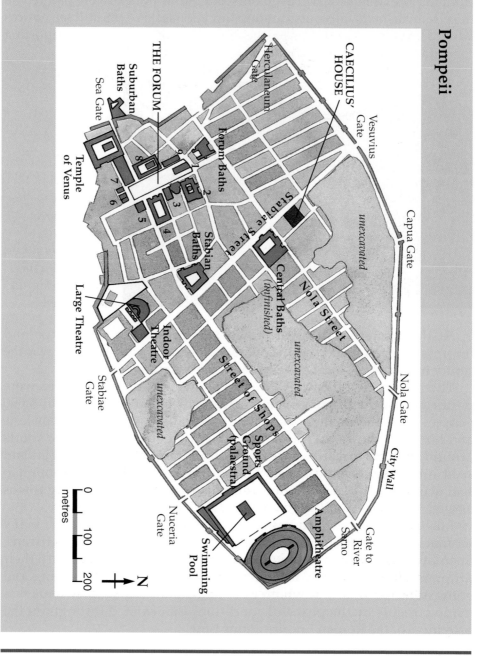

Buildings around the Forum:
1 Temple of Jupiter;
2 Market;
3 Temples of the Emperors and the Lares of Pompeii;
4 Eumachia's Clothworkers' Meeting Hall;
5 Polling Station;
6 Municipal Offices;
7 Basilica;
8 Temple of Apollo;
9 Vegetable Market and Public Toilet.

CAECILIUS' HOUSE

THE FORUM

Suburban Baths

Sea Gate

Temple of Venus

Herculaneum Gate

Forum Baths

Vesuvius Gate

Stabiae Street

Central Baths (unfinished)

Stabian Baths

Large Theatre

Indoor Theatre

Stabiae Gate

unexcavated

Nola Street

unexcavated

Street of Shops

Capua Gate

Nola Gate

City Wall

Gate to River Sarno

Amphitheatre

Swimming Pool

Sports Ground (palaestra)

unexcavated

Nuceria Gate

metres
0   100   200

N

The town's water supply was brought from the hills by an aqueduct; on reaching Pompeii, it was stored in large tanks on high ground at the northern side. The pressure created by the water in these tanks provided a good flow through underground lead pipes to all parts of the town, including the public baths. Public fountains, like this one in the Street of Shops, stood at many street corners. Most people drew their water from these, but wealthier citizens paid special rates for water piped directly into their homes.

From Britain in the northwest to Syria and Palestine in the east, Rome maintained peace and provided firm government. The frontiers of the empire were held secure by Roman troops stationed at important points. A system of well-built roads made travel by land relatively easy and provided an effective means of communication between Rome and distant parts of the empire. For many purposes, particularly for trade, travel by sea was more convenient. Ships carried cargoes of building materials, foodstuffs, and luxury goods across the Mediterranean; taxes were collected in the provinces. Pompeii was not a large town, but it played its part in the flourishing commercial and cultural life of the empire.

Streets of Pompeii

Here are some glimpses of the streets of Pompeii.

A plaster cast of shop shutters.

The sign from a dairy.

A section of wall covered with painted slogans.

Counters and wine storage jars (amphorae) are still in place in some of the bars and food shops.

Some bars have paintings on the walls showing the customers drinking and gambling.

Word Study

A Give the Latin word from which these words are derived:

1 provident
2 janitor
3 circumspect
4 proclamation
5 responsive
6 deportation
7 ridicule
8 magnanimous
9 irate
10 imbibe

B Select the word which does not come from the same root as the others:

1 advise   evident   visceral   supervise   interview
2 vine   vignette   vigilant   vintage   wine
3 insurgent   regional   resurrection   surge   resurgence
4 clamorous   reclamation   clamp   declaim   claimant
5 despondent   responsibility   correspond   sponge   sponsor

C Give the derivatives of **portat** suggested in the phrases below:

1 Easily carried: port----.
2 A means of carrying from one place to another:
   -----port-----.
3 Carrying a great deal of significance: --port---.
4 Furnishing assistance: ---port---.
5 A person who writes accounts of events: --port--.

Stage 3
Vocabulary Checklist

ad	*to*
bibit	*drinks*
circumspectat	*looks around*
clāmat	*shouts*
ecce!	*see! look!*
et	*and*
exit	*goes out*
exspectat	*waits for*
forum	*forum, business center*
iānua	*door*
īrātus	*angry*
leō	*lion*
magnus	*big, large, great*
nāvis	*ship*
nōn	*not*
portat	*carries*
respondet	*replies*
rīdet	*laughs, smiles*
salvē!	*hello!*
surgit	*gets up, rises*
taberna	*store, shop, inn*
videt	*sees*
vīlla	*house*
vīnum	*wine*

This painting shows Mercury, the god of profit as well as the messenger of the gods. It is painted above a cloth workshop in the Street of Shops, to bring success to the business.

IN FORO

Stage 4

1 Grumiō:
　　ego sum coquus.
　　ego cēnam coquō.

2 Caecilius:
　　ego sum argentārius.
　　ego pecūniam teneō.

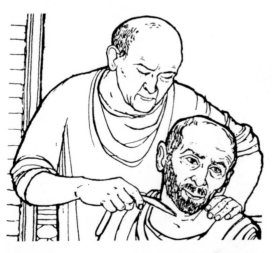

3 Pantagathus:
　　ego sum tōnsor.
　　ego barbam tondeō.

4 Syphāx:
    ego sum vēnālīcius.
    ego servum vēndō.

5 poēta:
    ego sum poēta.
    ego versum recitō.

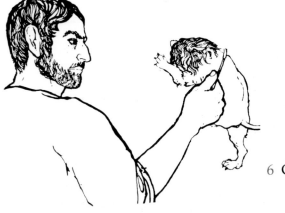

6 Celer:
    ego sum pictor.
    ego leōnem pingō.

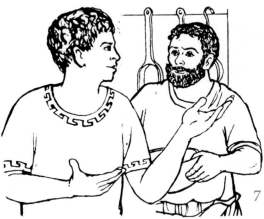

7 Quīntus: quid tū coquis?
   Grumiō: ego cēnam coquō.

8 Quīntus: quid tū tenēs?
   Caecilius: ego pecūniam teneō.

9 Quīntus: quid tū tondēs?
   tōnsor: ego barbam tondeō.

10 Quīntus: quid tū vēndis?
   vēnālīcius: ego servum vēndō.

11 Quīntus: quid tū recitās?
   poēta: ego versum recitō.

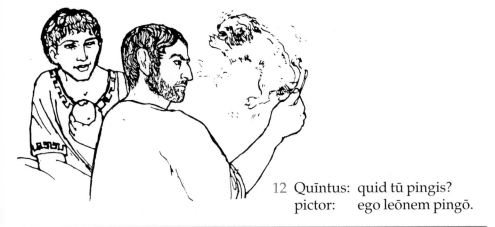

12 Quīntus: quid tū pingis?
   pictor: ego leōnem pingō.

13 Metella: quis es tū?
   ancilla: ego sum Melissa.

14 Metella: quis es tū?
   vēnālīcius: ego sum Syphāx.

15 Metella: quis es tū?
   tonsor: ego sum Pantagathus.

Hermogenēs

Caecilius est in forō. Caecilius in forō argentāriam habet. Hermogenēs ad forum venit. Hermogenēs est mercātor Graecus. mercātor nāvem habet. mercātor Caecilium salūtat.

"ego sum mercātor Graecus," inquit Hermogenēs. "ego sum mercātor probus. ego pecūniam quaerō." 5

"cūr tū pecūniam quaeris?" inquit Caecilius. "tū nāvem habēs."

"sed nāvis nōn adest," respondet Hermogenēs. "nāvis est in Graeciā. ego pecūniam nōn habeō. ego tamen sum probus. ego semper pecūniam reddō."

"ecce!" inquit Caecilius. "ego cēram habeō. tū ānulum habēs?" 10

"ego ānulum habeō," respondet Hermogenēs. "ānulus signum habet. ecce! ego signum in cērā imprimō."

Caecilius pecūniam trādit. mercātor pecūniam capit et ē forō currit.

ēheu! Hermogenēs nōn revenit. mercātor pecūniam nōn reddit. 15
Caecilius Hermogenem ad basilicam vocat.

argentāriam	*banker's stall*		**cēram**	*wax tablet*
Graecus	*Greek*		**ānulum**	*ring*
probus	*honest*		**signum**	*seal, sign*
cūr?	*why?*		**ego imprimō**	*I press*
nōn adest	*is not here*		**trādit**	*hands over*
in Graeciā	*in Greece*		**capit**	*takes*
tamen	*however*		**currit**	*runs*
semper	*always*		**ad basilicam**	*to the law court*
ego reddō	*I give back*			

A corner of the forum with shops opening off the colonnade.

in basilicā

iūdex basilicam intrat.

iūdex:	quis es tū?
Caecilius:	ego sum Lūcius Caecilius Iūcundus.
iūdex:	tū es Pompēiānus?
Caecilius:	ego sum Pompēiānus. 5
iūdex:	quid tū in urbe agis?
Caecilius:	ego cotīdiē ad forum veniō. ego sum argentārius.
iūdex:	cūr tū hodiē ad basilicam venīs?
Caecilius:	Hermogenēs multam pecūniam dēbet.
	Hermogenēs pecūniam nōn reddit. 10
Hermogenēs:	Caecilius est mendāx!
iūdex:	quis es tū?
Hermogenēs:	ego sum Hermogenēs.
iūdex:	Hermogenēs, quid tū in urbe agis?
Hermogenēs:	ego in forō negōtium agō. ego sum mercātor. 15
iūdex:	quid tū respondēs? tū pecūniam dēbēs?
Hermogenēs:	ego pecūniam nōn dēbeō. amīcus meus est testis.
amīcus:	ego sum testis. Hermogenēs pecūniam nōn dēbet.
	Caecilius est mendāx.
Caecilius:	tū, Hermogenēs, es mendāx. amīcus tuus quoque 20
	est mendāx. tū pecūniam nōn reddis …
iūdex:	satis! tū Hermogenem accūsās, sed tū rem nōn
	probās.
Caecilius:	ego cēram habeō. tū signum in cērā vidēs.
Hermogenēs:	ēheu! 25
iūdex:	Hermogenēs, tū ānulum habēs?
Caecilius:	ecce! Hermogenēs ānulum cēlat.
iūdex:	ubi est ānulus? ecce! ānulus rem probat. ego
	Hermogenem convincō.

iūdex	*judge*	**meus**	*my, mine*
quis?	*who?*	**testis**	*witness*
Pompēiānus	*a citizen of*	**tuus**	*your*
	Pompeii, Pompeian	**tū accūsās**	*you accuse*
quid tū agis?	*what do you do?*	**tū rem nōn probās**	*you do not*
in urbe	*in the city*		*prove the case*
cotīdiē	*every day*	**cēlat**	*is hiding*
hodiē	*today*	**ubi?**	*where?*
dēbet	*owes*	**ego convincō**	*I convict,*
mendāx	*liar*		*I find guilty*

About the Language

A In the first three Stages, you met sentences like this:

> ancilla ambulat.   mercātor sedet.   servus currit.
> *The slave-girl walks.   The merchant sits.   The slave runs.*

All of these sentences have a noun (**ancilla**, **mercātor**, **servus**) and a word indicating the action of the sentence, known as the **verb**. In the sentences above the verbs are **ambulat**, **sedet**, **currit**.

In all the sentences you met in the first three Stages, the verb ended in -t.

B In Stage 4, you have met sentences with **ego** and **tū**:

> **ego** ambulō. *I walk.*   **ego** sedeō. *I sit.*   **ego** currō. *I run.*
> **tū** ambulās. *You walk.*   **tū** sedēs. *You sit.*   **tū** curris.*You run.*

C Notice the three different forms of each word:

> ego ambulō.   ego sedeō.   ego currō.
> tū ambulās.   tū sedēs.   tū curris.
> ancilla ambulat.   mercātor sedet.   servus currit.

Notice also that the words **ego** and **tū** are not strictly necessary, since the endings **-ō** and **-s** make it clear that *I* and *you* are performing the action of the sentence. The Romans generally used **ego** and **tū** only for emphasis.

D The following example is rather different:

> ego **sum** īrātus.   tū **es** īrātus.   servus **est** īrātus.
> *I am angry.*   *You are angry.*   *The slave is angry.*

E Further examples:

1 Caecilius recitat. ego recitō.
2 Quīntus dormit. tū dormīs.
3 tū labōrās. servus labōrat.
4 Syphāx servum habet. ego servum habeō.
5 ego pecūniam trādō. tū pecūniam trādis.
6 Pantagathus est tōnsor. tū es mercātor. ego sum poēta.
7 ambulō; circumspectō; circumspectās; es.
8 sum; audiō; audīs; habēs.

Practicing the Language

A Write out each pair of sentences, completing the second sentence with the correct verb from the parentheses. Translate both sentences.

1 ego sum mercātor. ego nāvem (stō, habeō).
2 ego sum servus. ego in culīnā (habeō, labōrō).
3 tū es ancilla. tū suāviter (venīs, cantās).
4 tū es mendāx. tū pecūniam (dēbēs, ambulās).
5 ego sum Syphāx. ego ancillam (vēndō, ambulō).

B Write out each pair of sentences, completing the second sentence with the correct verb from the parentheses. Translate both sentences.

1 ego sum coquus. ego cēnam (coquō, coquis, coquit).
2 ego sum Herculēs. ego fūstem (tenēs, tenet, teneō).
3 tū es amīcus. tū vīllam (intrō, intrās, intrat).
4 tū es iūdex. tū Hermogenem (convincit, convincis, convincō).
5 Syphāx est vēnālīcius. Syphāx ancillam (vēndō, vēndis, vēndit).

C Choose the correct form for the word in parentheses. Then translate the sentence.

1 (argentārius, argentārium) in forō sedet.
2 Caecilius (mercātōrem, mercātor) salūtat.
3 "(nāvem, nāvis) nōn adest," inquit Hermogenēs. "quid quaeris?" inquit Caecilius.
4 "(pecūnia, pecūniam) quaerō," respondet mercātor Graecus.
5 Caecilius pecūniam trādit, sed Hermogenēs nōn est (probus, probum).
6 quis est mendāx? (Hermogenem, Hermogenēs) est mendāx.
7 iūdex (ānulus, ānulum) videt.

D Translate into English:

Grumiō et leō

Celer in vīllā labōrat. Celer pictūram in triclīniō pingit. magnus leō est in pictūrā. Celer ē vīllā discēdit.

Grumiō ē tabernā revenit et vīllam intrat. Grumiō est ēbrius. Grumiō pictūram videt. Grumiō est perterritus.

"ēheu!" inquit Grumiō. "leō est in triclīniō. leō mē spectat. 5 leō mē ferōciter petit."

Grumiō ē triclīniō currit et culīnam intrat. Clēmēns est in culīnā. Clēmēns Grumiōnem spectat.

"cūr tū es perterritus?" inquit Clēmēns.

"ēheu! leō est in triclīniō," inquit Grumiō. 10

"ita vērō," respondet Clēmēns, "et servus ēbrius est in culīnā."

discēdit	*departs, leaves*
ē tabernā	*from the inn*
ēbrius	*drunk*
ita vērō	*yes*

The basilica (law court) was a large, long building with rows of pillars inside and a high platform at the far end on which the town's senior officials may have sat when hearing lawsuits.

The Forum

The forum was the heart of the commercial, administrative, and religious life of Pompeii. It was a large open space surrounded on three sides by a colonnade, with various important buildings grouped closely around it. The open area, 156 yards (143 meters) long and 42 yards (38 meters) wide, was paved with stone. In it stood a number of statues commemorating the emperor, members of the emperor's family, and local citizens who had given distinguished service to the town.

The illustration below shows a typical scene in the forum. The merchant on the left has set up his wooden stall and is selling small articles of ironware, pincers, knives, and hammers; the merchant on the right is a shoemaker. He

Part of the colonnade, which had two stories, seen from inside. You can see the holes for the floor beams of the top story.

has seated his customers on stools while he shows them his goods. Behind the merchants is the colonnade. This elegant structure, supported by columns of white marble, provided an open corridor in which people could walk and do business, protected from the heat of the sun in summer and the rain in winter. On the right, behind the shoemaker, is a statue of an important citizen mounted on horseback. Behind it is one of the bronze gates through which people entered the forum. The whole

Drawing based on another part of the painting opposite, which is unfortunately not well preserved.

Reading the notice-boards.

forum area was a pedestrian precinct, and a row of upright stones at each entrance provided an effective barrier to wheeled traffic. You can see two of these stones in the picture on page 51.

In the Pompeian wall-painting above, you see a public notice-board fixed across the pedestals of three statues and some people studying the bulletins. There were no newspapers in Pompeii, but certain kinds of information, such as election results and dates of processions, festivals, and shows, had to be publicized. This was done by putting up notice-boards in the forum.

In addition to official announcements, a large number of graffiti have been found in the forum and elsewhere in which ordinary citizens recorded lost property, announced accommodations for rent, left lovers' messages, and publicized the problems they were having with their neighbors. One example reads:

> **A bronze jar has been lost from this shop. A reward is offered for its recovery.**

Another complains of noise at night and asks the aedile (the official who was responsible for policing) to do something about it:

> **Macerior requests the aedile to stop people from making a noise in the streets and disturbing decent folk who are asleep.**

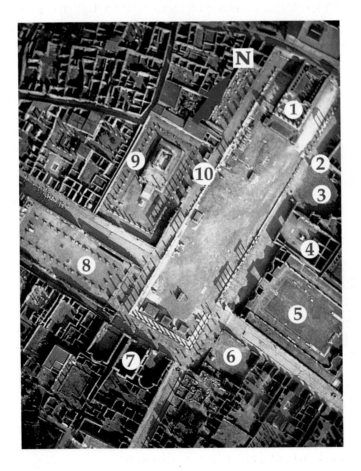

Aerial view of the forum.

Some of the most important public buildings were situated around the forum. In a prominent position at the north end stood the Temple of Jupiter, the greatest of the Roman gods (see 1). It was probably from the steps of this temple that political speeches were made at election times. Speeches and announcements could also be made from a special platform in the forum called the tribunal.

To the west of the Temple of Jupiter, beneath the colonnade, were the prison and the public latrines. Just behind the temple stood a set of public baths.

Next to the temple, in the northeast corner of the forum, was a large covered market (2) which contained permanent shops rather than temporary stalls. The storekeepers here sold mainly meat, fish, and vegetables. On the other side of the forum a public weights and measures table (10) ensured that they gave fair measures.

Immediately to the south of the market was a temple dedicated to the **larēs**, the guardian spirits of Pompeii (3), and next to that stood a temple in honor of the Roman emperors (4). Across the forum was the Temple of Apollo (9), and near the southwest corner of the forum was the Temple of Venus, an important goddess for the Pompeians, who believed that she took a special interest in their town.

We have now mentioned five religious shrines around or near the forum. There were many others elsewhere in the town, including a temple of the goddess Isis, whose worship had been brought to Italy from Egypt. The Pompeians believed in many gods, rather than one, and it seemed to them quite natural to believe that different gods should care for different parts of human life. Apollo, for example, was associated with medicine, music, and prophecy; Venus was the goddess of love and beauty.

On the east side of the forum was the Clothworkers' Meeting Hall (5), whose porch and colonnade were built with money given by Eumachia (see illustration on page 12), a successful businesswoman and priestess. As this was one of the most prosperous industries in the town, it is not surprising that its headquarters were large and occupied such a prominent site.

Next to the meeting hall of the clothworkers was the polling station (6), an open building where voting in the municipal elections took place. Along the south side were three municipal offices (7), perhaps used for the treasury, the record office, and the meeting room of the town council.

At the southwest corner stood the **basilica**, or courthouse (8). This was a large, long building with two rows of interior columns marking side aisles. At one end was a high platform on which the two senior officials, called **duovirī**, may have sat when hearing lawsuits. The basilica was also used as a meeting place for businessmen.

Carving from Eumachia's Meeting Hall.

Forum – Focus of Life

Business, religion, local government: these were the official purposes of the forum and its surrounding buildings. This great crowded square was the center of much of the open-air life in Pompeii. Here people gathered to do business, to shop, or to meet friends. Strangers visiting the forum would have been struck by its size, the splendid buildings surrounding it, and the general air of prosperity.

The Temple of Jupiter.

The Temple of Apollo.

The Market.

Municipal Offices.

The Weights and Measures Table.

The Temple of the Emperors.

Word Study

A Give the Latin word from which each of these words is derived:

1 query
2 render
3 egotistical
4 prejudicial
5 agile
6 biscuit
7 resignation
8 insatiable
9 mendacious
10 invocation

B Match each word to its correct definition listed below:

advocate   impecunious   terrify
agent   judicial   vendor
exhibit   satisfy

1 ..... to fulfill
2 ..... a person who sells something
3 ..... a defender or supporter
4 ..... pertaining to legal practice
5 ..... a person who acts on another's behalf
6 ..... to frighten
7 ..... having little money, poor
8 ..... to have out on display

Some seal-stones from rings and
a gold seal-ring without a stone.
The stone on the left is enlarged.

Stage 4
Vocabulary Checklist

agit	does
negōtium agit	does business, works
ānulus	ring
cēra	wax, wax tablet
coquit	cooks
cūr?	why?
ē, ex	out of, from
ego	I
ēheu!	alas! oh dear!
habet	has
inquit	says
iūdex: iūdicem	judge
mendāx: mendācem	liar
pecūnia	money
perterritus	terrified
poēta	poet
quaerit	searches for, looks for
quis?	who?
reddit	gives back
satis	enough
sed	but
signum	sign, seal, signal
tū	you
vēndit	sells
vocat	calls

This marble carving was found in Caecilius' house. It shows the Temple of Jupiter, with statues of men on horseback on each side, as it looked during an earthquake that happened in A.D. 62.

IN THEATRO

Stage 5

in viā

1 canis est in viā.

2 canēs sunt in viā.

3 servus est in viā.

4 servī sunt in viā.

5 puella est in viā.

6 puellae sunt in viā.

7 puer est in viā.

8 puerī sunt in viā.

9 mercātor est in viā.

10 mercātōrēs sunt in viā.

in theātrō

11 spectātor in theātrō sedet.

12 spectātōrēs in theātrō sedent.

13 āctor in scaenā stat.

14 āctōrēs in scaenā stant.

15 fēmina spectat.

16 fēminae spectant.

17 senex dormit.

18 senēs dormiunt.

19 iuvenis plaudit.

20 iuvenēs plaudunt.

āctōrēs

magna turba est in urbe. fēminae et puellae sunt in turbā. senēs
quoque et iuvenēs sunt in turbā. servī hodiē nōn labōrant. senēs
hodiē nōn dormiunt. mercātōrēs hodiē nōn sunt occupātī.
Pompēiānī sunt ōtiōsī. urbs tamen nōn est quiēta. Pompēiānī ad
theātrum contendunt. magnus clāmor est in urbe.   5

   agricolae urbem intrant. nautae urbem petunt. pāstōrēs dē
monte veniunt et ad urbem contendunt. turba per portam ruit.

   nūntius in forō clāmat: "āctōrēs
sunt in urbe. āctōrēs sunt in
theātrō. Priscus fābulam dat.   10
Priscus fābulam bonam dat.
āctōrēs sunt Actius et Sorex."

   Caecilius et Metella ē vīllā
discēdunt. argentārius et uxor ad
theātrum ambulant. Clēmēns et   15
Melissa ad theātrum contendunt.
sed Grumiō in vīllā manet.

āctōrēs	actors
turba	crowd
fēminae	women
puellae	girls
iuvenēs	young men
ōtiōsī	at leisure, with time off, idle
quiēta	quiet
ad theātrum	to the theater
contendunt	hurry
clāmor	shout, uproar
agricolae	farmers
nautae	sailors
petunt	head for, seek
pāstōrēs	shepherds
dē monte	down from the mountain
per portam	through the gate
ruit	rushes
nūntius	messenger
fābulam dat	is putting on a play
uxor	wife
manet	remains, stays

Two actors in mask and costume.
These statues were found in a
garden in a house in Pompeii.

About the Language I

A In the first four Stages, you have met sentences like these:

puella sedet.   servus labōrat.
The girl is sitting.   *The slave is working.*

leō currit.   mercātor dormit.
The lion is running.   *The merchant is sleeping.*

Sentences like these refer to **one** person or thing, and in each sentence the form of both words (the noun and the verb) is said to be **singular**.

B Sentences which refer to **more than one** person or thing use a different form of the words known as the **plural**. Compare the singular and plural forms in the following sentences:

singular	*plural*
puella labōrat.	puellae labōrant.
The girl is working.	*The girls are working.*
servus rīdet.	servī rīdent.
The slave is laughing.	*The slaves are laughing.*
leō currit.	leōnēs currunt.
The lion is running.	*The lions are running.*
mercātor dormit.	mercātōrēs dormiunt.
The merchant is sleeping.	*The merchants are sleeping.*

Note that in each of these sentences **both** the noun and the verb show the difference between singular and plural.

C Look again at the sentences in section B and note the difference between the singular and plural forms of the verb.

singular	*plural*
labōrat	labōrant
rīdet	rīdent
currit	currunt
dormit	dormiunt

In each case the singular ending is **-t** and the plural ending is **-nt**.

D Notice how Latin shows the difference between *is* and *are* .

> mercātor **est** in viā. mercātōrēs **sunt** in viā.
> *The merchant is in the street.* *The merchants are in the street.*

E Further examples:

1. amīcus ambulat. amīcī ambulant.
2. āctor clāmat. āctōrēs clāmant.
3. fēminae plaudunt. fēmina plaudit.
4. vēnālīciī intrant. vēnālīcius intrat.
5. ancilla respondet. ancillae respondent.
6. senēs dormiunt. senex dormit.

Fragment of wall-painting showing an actor in the dressing-room, studying his mask.

Poppaea

Poppaea est ancilla. ancilla prope iānuam stat. ancilla viam spectat. dominus in hortō dormit. dominus est Lucriō. Lucriō est senex.

Poppaea:	ego amīcum meum exspectō. ubi est amīcus?	
	(*Lucriō stertit.*)	
	ēheu! Lucriō est in vīllā.	5
	(*agricolae in viā clāmant.*)	
agricolae:	euge! agricolae hodiē nōn labōrant!	
Poppaea:	Lucriō! Lucriō! agricolae urbem intrant. agricolae adsunt.	
Lucriō:	(*sēmisomnus*) a … a … agricolae?	10
puerī:	euge! Sorex! Actius! āctōrēs adsunt.	
Poppaea:	Lucriō! Lucriō! puerī per viam currunt.	
Lucriō:	quid tū clāmās, Poppaea? cūr tū clāmōrem facis?	
Poppaea:	Lucriō, Pompēiānī clāmōrem faciunt. agricolae et puerī sunt in viā.	15
Lucriō:	cūr tū mē vexās?	
Poppaea:	āctōrēs in theātrō fābulam agunt.	
Lucriō:	āctōrēs?	
Poppaea:	Sorex et Actius adsunt.	
Lucriō:	quid tū dīcis?	20
Poppaea:	(*īrāta*) senēs ad theātrum ambulant, iuvenēs ad theātrum contendunt, omnēs Pompēiānī ad theātrum ruunt. āctōrēs in theātrō fābulam agunt.	
Lucriō:	euge! āctōrēs adsunt. ego quoque ad theātrum contendō.	25
	(*exit Lucriō. amīcus vīllam intrat.*)	
amīcus:	salvē! mea columba!	
Poppaea:	Grumiō, dēliciae meae! salvē!	
Grumiō:	ubi est dominus tuus?	
Poppaea:	Lucriō abest.	30
Grumiō:	euge!	

euge!	*hurrah!*	**fābulam agunt**	*act in a play*
adsunt	*are here*	**tū dīcis**	*you say*
sēmisomnus	*half-asleep*	**omnēs**	*all*
puerī	*boys*	**mea columba**	*my dove*
tū … facis	*you make*	**dēliciae meae**	*my darling*
clāmōrem	*a noise*	**abest**	*is out*
tū … vexās	*you annoy*		

About the Language II

A Study the following examples of singular and plural forms:

singular	*plural*
puella rīdet.	**puellae** rīdent.
The girl is smiling.	*The girls are smiling.*
servus ambulat.	**servī** ambulant.
The slave is walking.	*The slaves are walking.*
mercātor contendit.	**mercātōrēs** contendunt.
The merchant is hurrying.	*The merchants are hurrying.*

B Each of the nouns in bold type is in the nominative case, because it refers to a person or persons who are performing some action, such as walking or smiling.

C **puella**, **servus**, and **mercātor** are therefore **nominative singular**, and **puellae**, **servī**, and **mercātōrēs** are **nominative plural**.

D Notice the forms of the nominative plural in the different declensions:

first declension	*second declension*	*third declension*
puellae	servī	mercātōrēs
ancillae	amīcī	leōnēs
fēminae	puerī	senēs

The Pompeians often used theatrical images to decorate their homes.

Practicing the Language

A Write out each sentence, completing it with the correct form of the verb in the parentheses. Then translate the sentence.

1 āctōrēs (adest, adsunt).
2 puellae in theātrō (sedent, sedet).
3 agricola ad urbem (currunt, currit).
4 Pompēiānī clāmōrem (facit, faciunt).
5 servī ad theātrum (contendit, contendunt).
6 pater (est, sunt) in tablīnō.

B Write out each sentence, completing it with the correct singular or plural noun in the parentheses. Then translate the sentence.

1 (pāstor, pāstōrēs) ad theātrum contendunt.
2 (puella, puellae) āctōrem laudat.
3 (vēnālīcius, vēnālīciī) ad urbem veniunt.
4 (fēmina, fēminae) fābulam spectant.
5 (senex, senēs) in forō dormit.
6 (puer, puerī) in urbe sunt.

C Write out each sentence, completing it with the correct form of the noun in the parentheses. Then translate the sentence.

1 omnēs Pompēiānī (āctōrem, āctor) spectant.
2 Grumiō (cēna optima, cēnam optimam) coquit.
3 (senem, senex) fābulam dat.
4 Caecilius (ancillam, ancilla) quaerit.
5 agricolae (clāmor, clāmōrem) faciunt.
6 puellae (Cerberus, Cerberum) audiunt.

D Translate into English:

in theātrō

hodiē Pompēiānī sunt ōtiōsī. dominī et servī nōn labōrant.
multī Pompēiānī in theātrō sedent. spectātōrēs Actium
exspectant. tandem Actius in scaenā stat. Pompēiānī
plaudunt.

    subitō Pompēiānī magnum clāmōrem audiunt. servus   *5*
theātrum intrat. "euge! fūnambulus adest," clāmat servus.
Pompēiānī Actium nōn spectant. omnēs Pompēiānī ē theātrō
currunt et fūnambulum spectant.

    nēmō in theātrō manet. Actius tamen nōn est īrātus. Actius
quoque fūnambulum spectat.   *10*

multī	*many*
spectātōrēs	*spectators*
tandem	*at last*
in scaenā	*on stage*
plaudunt	*applaud, clap*
subitō	*suddenly*
fūnambulus	*tightrope walker*
nēmō	*no one*

This tightrope walker from a wall-painting is a satyr, one of the followers of Bacchus, god of wine. He has a tail and plays the double pipes.

The Theater at Pompeii

Plays were not performed in Pompeii every day but only at festivals, which were held several times a year. There was, therefore, all the more excitement in the town when the notices appeared announcing a performance. On the day itself, the stores were closed, and no business was done in the forum. Men and women with their slaves set off for the theater early in the morning. Some carried cushions because the seats were made of stone, and many took food and drink for the day. The only people who did not need to hurry were the members of the town council and other important citizens, for whom the best seats at the front of the auditorium were reserved. These important people carried tokens which indicated the entrance they should use and where they were to sit. Latecomers among the ordinary citizens had to be content with a seat right at the top of the large semicircular auditorium. The large open-air theater at Pompeii could hold 5,000 people. Adjoining it was the **Odeon**, a smaller, more elegant, roofed theater.

The large Pompeian theater was modelled on the Greek and had essentially the same parts. The **cavea**, or seating area, was a semicircular sloping auditorium in which seats rose in tiers. The **orchēstra** in Pompeii was horseshoe-shaped and provided seating space for important officials. Behind the **scaena**, or stage, was a building (**scaenae frōns**) as high as the auditorium. The *scaenae frōns* had three or five doorways, and the entire front was decorated with columns and niches.

Pompeii's elegant, smaller, roofed theater.

A bronze head of Sorex, a famous actor of Pompeii. Originally the eyes would have been inserted in lifelike colors.

Pompeii's main, open-air theater.

A dramatic performance was a public occasion, and admission to the theater was free. All the expenses were paid by a wealthy citizen, who provided the actors, the producer, the scenery, and the costumes. He volunteered to do this not only to benefit his fellow citizens but also to gain political popularity which would be useful in local elections.

The performance consisted of a series of plays and lasted all day, even during the heat of the afternoon. To keep the spectators cool, a large canvas awning was suspended by ropes and pulleys across most of the large theater. The awning was managed by sailors, who were used to handling ropes and canvas. Even so, on a windy day, the awning could not be unfurled, and the audience had to make use of hats or sunshades to protect themselves from the sun. Between plays, scented water was sprinkled by attendants.

One of the most popular kinds of production was the pantomime, a mixture of opera and ballet. The plot, which was usually serious, was taken from the Greek myths. The parts of the different characters were mimed and danced by one masked performer, while a chorus sang the lyrics. An orchestra containing such instruments as the lyre, double pipes, trumpet, and castanets accompanied the performance, providing a rhythmical beat. Pantomime actors were usually Greek slaves or freedmen. They were much admired for their skill and stamina and attracted a large following of fans.

Equally popular were the comic actors. The bronze statue of one of these, Sorex, was discovered at Pompeii, together with graffiti on walls naming other popular actors. One of these reads:

Actius, our favorite, come back quickly.

Comic actors appeared in vulgar farces and in short one-act plays which were often put on at the end of longer performances. These short plays were about Italian country life and were packed with rude jokes and slapstick. They used just a few familiar characters, such as Pappus, an old fool, and Manducus, a greedy clown. These characters were instantly recognizable from the strange masks worn by the actors. The Roman poet Juvenal describes a performance of a play of this kind in a country theater, where the children sitting on their mothers' laps shrank back in horror when they saw the gaping, white masks. These masks, like those used in other plays, were probably made of linen which was covered with plaster and painted.

A clay model of a mask, perhaps for the character Manducus.

Sometimes, at a festival, the comedies of Plautus and Terence, playwrights of the second century B.C., were put on. These plays also used a number of familiar characters, but the plots were complicated and the dialogue more witty than that of the farces.

A mosaic of a theater musician.

The Comedies of Plautus

There is usually a young man from a respectable family who is leading a wild life; he is often in debt and in love with a pretty, but unsuitable, slave-girl. His father, who is old-fashioned and disapproving, has to be kept in the dark by deception. The son is usually helped in this by a cunning slave, who gets himself and his young master in and out of trouble at great speed. Eventually, it is discovered that the girl is free-born and from a good family. The young man is, therefore, able to marry his true love, and all ends happily.

1 *Father has to be restrained from violence when he finds his son coming home drunk from a party. The cunning slave props the lad up. A musician is playing the double pipes.*

2 *The boy has been with his beloved slave-girl (here's her mask).*

3 *The slave sits on an altar for sanctuary, hoping to escape terrible punishment.*

4 *The slave uncovers a basket in the girl's possession and finds her baby clothes – they are recognized! She must be the long-lost daughter of father's best friend and wrongly enslaved by pirates! All live happily ever after.*

Word Study

A Match each word to its correct definition listed below:

audience   feminine   state
convene   rejuvenate   turbulent
fabulous   spectator   ubiquitous

1 ..... a group of listeners
2 ..... mythical or legendary; marvelous
3 ..... a condition or situation
4 ..... to assemble, gather together
5 ..... a person who watches
6 ..... rowdy, unruly
7 ..... characteristic of women
8 ..... to make young again
9 ..... appearing everywhere

B Select the word which does not come from the same root as the others:

1 cursor cursive curriculum curse occur
2 petulant perpetual petition appetite petroleum
3 circumvent ventilate adventure conventional inventive
4 specimen conspicuous speck introspective despise

A musical interlude in a play.

Stage 5
Vocabulary Checklist

adest	*is here*
adsunt	*are here*
agricola	*farmer*
ambulat	*walks*
audit	*hears, listens to*
clāmor: clāmōrem	*shout, uproar*
contendit	*hurries*
currit	*runs*
euge!	*hurrah!*
fābula	*play, story*
fābulam agit	*acts in a play*
fēmina	*woman*
hodiē	*today*
iuvenis:iuvenem	*young man*
meus	*my, mine*
multus	*much*
multī	*many*
optimus	*very good, excellent, best*
petit	*heads for, attacks, seeks*
plaudit	*applauds, claps*
puella	*girl*
senex: senem	*old man*
spectat	*looks at, watches*
stat	*stands*
turba	*crowd*
ubi?	*where?*
urbs: urbem	*city*
venit	*comes*

Sculpture of a theater mask.

FELIX

Stage 6

1 servī per viam ambulābant.

2 canis subitō lātrāvit.

3 Grumiō canem timēbat.

4 "pestis!" clāmāvit coquus.

5 Clēmēns erat fortis.

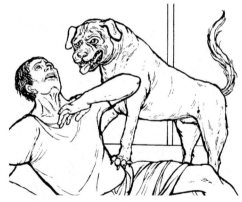
6 sed canis Clēmentem superāvit.

7 Quīntus per viam ambulābat.

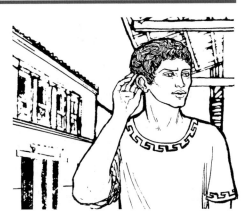

8 iuvenis clāmōrem audīvit.

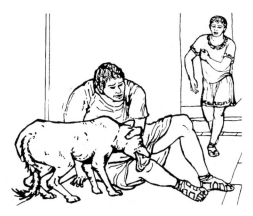

9 canis Clēmentem vexābat.

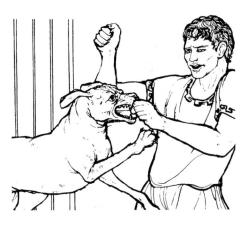

10 Quīntus canem pulsāvit.

11 servī erant laetī.

12 servī Quīntum laudāvērunt.

pugna

Clēmēns in forō ambulābat. turba maxima erat in forō. servī et ancillae cibum emēbant. multī pistōrēs pānem vēndēbant. poēta recitābat. mercātor Graecus contentiōnem cum agricolā habēbat. mercātor īrātus pecūniam postulābat. subitō agricola Graecum pulsāvit, quod Graecus agricolam vituperābat. Pompēiānī 5 rīdēbant, et agricolam incitābant. Clēmēns, postquam clāmōrem audīvit, ad pugnam festīnāvit. tandem agricola mercātōrem superāvit et ē forō agitāvit. Pompēiānī agricolam fortem laudāvērunt.

pugna	*fight*	**pulsāvit**	*hit, punched*
maxima	*very large*	**quod**	*because*
erat	*was*	**incitābant**	*were urging on*
pistōrēs	*bakers*	**postquam**	*when, after*
pānem	*bread*	**festīnāvit**	*hurried*
contentiōnem	*argument*	**superāvit**	*overpowered*
cum agricolā	*with a farmer*	**agitāvit**	*chased*
postulābat	*was demanding*		

Shopping for dinner.

Fēlīx

multī Pompēiānī in tabernā vīnum bibēbant. Clēmēns tabernam
intrāvit. subitō Clēmēns "Fēlīx!" clāmāvit. Clēmēns Fēlīcem laetē
salūtāvit. Fēlīx erat lībertus.

Clēmēns Fēlīcem ad vīllam invītāvit. Clēmēns et Fēlīx vīllam
intrāvērunt. Clēmēns Caecilium et Metellam quaesīvit. Caecilius 5
in tablīnō scrībēbat. Metella in hortō sedēbat. Caecilius et Metella
ad ātrium festīnāvērunt et Fēlīcem salūtāvērunt. postquam
Quīntus ātrium intrāvit, Fēlīx iuvenem spectāvit. lībertus erat
valdē commōtus. paene lacrimābat; sed rīdēbat.

tum Clēmēns ad culīnam festīnāvit. Grumiō in culīnā 10
dormiēbat. Clēmēns coquum excitāvit et tōtam rem nārrāvit.
coquus, quod erat laetus, cēnam optimam parāvit.

laetē	*happily*
lībertus	*freedman*
invītāvit	*invited*
valdē	*very much, very*
commōtus	*moved, affected*
paene	*almost*
lacrimābat	*was crying*
tum	*then*
excitāvit	*woke up, aroused*
tōtam rem	*the whole story*
nārrāvit	*told*
parāvit	*prepared*

Fēlīx et fūr

post cēnam Quīntus rogāvit, "pater, cūr Fēlīx nunc est lībertus? ōlim erat
servus tuus."
    tum pater tōtam rem nārrāvit.

Caecilius:	Fēlīx ōlim in tablīnō scrībēbat. Fēlīx erat sōlus.
	Clēmēns et Grumiō cibum in forō quaerēbant. 5
	Metella aberat, quod sorōrem vīsitābat.
Fēlīx:	pater tuus aberat, quod argentāriam in forō
	administrābat.
Caecilius:	nēmō erat in vīllā nisi Fēlīx et īnfāns. parvus īnfāns in
	cubiculō dormiēbat. subitō fūr per iānuam intrāvit. 10
	fūr tacitē ātrium circumspectāvit; tacitē cubiculum
	intrāvit, ubi īnfāns erat. Fēlīx nihil audīvit, quod
	intentē labōrābat. fūr parvum īnfantem ē vīllā tacitē
	portābat. subitō īnfāns vāgīvit. Fēlīx, postquam
	clāmōrem audīvit, statim ē tablīnō festīnāvit. 15
	"furcifer!" clāmāvit Fēlīx īrātus, et fūrem ferōciter
	pulsāvit. Fēlīx fūrem paene necāvit. ita Fēlīx parvum
	īnfantem servāvit.
Fēlīx:	dominus, postquam rem audīvit, erat laetus et mē
	līberāvit. ego igitur sum lībertus. 20
Quīntus:	sed quis erat īnfāns?
Caecilius:	erat Quīntus!

fūr	*thief*	**in cubiculō**	*in a bedroom*
post	*after*	**tacitē**	*quietly*
rogāvit	*asked*	**ubi**	*where*
nunc	*now*	**nihil**	*nothing*
ōlim	*once, some time ago*	**portābat**	*began to carry*
sōlus	*alone*	**vāgīvit**	*cried, wailed*
aberat	*was out*	**statim**	*at once*
sorōrem	*sister*	**necāvit**	*killed*
administrābat	*was looking after*	**ita**	*in this way*
nisi	*except*	**servāvit**	*saved*
īnfāns	*child, baby*	**līberāvit**	*freed, set free*
parvus	*little, small*	**igitur**	*therefore, and so*

About the Language

A All the stories in the first five Stages were set in the present, and in every sentence the verbs were in the **present tense**. Study the following examples:

PRESENT TENSE

singular servus **labōrat**. *The slave works* or *The slave is working.*
plural   servī **labōrant**. *The slaves work* or *The slaves are working.*

B In Stage 6, because the stories happened in the past, you have met the **imperfect tense** and the **perfect tense**. Study the different endings of the two past tenses and their English translation:

IMPERFECT TENSE

singular	poēta **recitābat**.	*A poet was reciting.*
	Metella in hortō **sedēbat**.	*Metella was sitting in the garden.*
plural	servī in forō **ambulābant**.	*The slaves were walking in the forum.*
	Pompēiānī vīnum **bibēbant**.	*The Pompeians were drinking wine.*

PERFECT TENSE

singular	coquus **intrāvit**.	*The cook entered.*
	Clēmēns clāmōrem **audīvit**.	*Clemens heard the uproar.*
plural	amīcī Caecilium **salūtāvērunt**.	*The friends greeted Caecilius.*
	iuvenēs ad tabernam **festīnāvērunt**.	*The young men hurried to an inn.*

C Compare the endings of the imperfect and perfect tenses with the endings of the present tense.

	singular	*plural*
PRESENT	portat	portant
IMPERFECT	portābat	portābant
PERFECT	portāvit	portāvērunt

You can see that in the imperfect and perfect tenses, as with the present tense, the singular ends in **-t** and the plural in **-nt**.

D Notice how Latin shows the difference between *is, are,* and *was, were.*

	singular	*plural*
PRESENT	Caecilius **est** in tablīnō.	servī **sunt** in culinā.
	Caecilius is in the study.	*The slaves are in the kitchen.*
IMPERFECT	Caecilius **erat** in forō.	servī **erant** in viā.
	Caecilius was in the forum.	*The slaves were in the street.*

E In the following examples you will see that the imperfect tense is often used of an action or situation which was going on for some time.

īnfāns in cubiculō **dormiēbat**.   pater et māter **aberant**.
The baby was sleeping in the   *The father and mother were*
bedroom.   *away.*

F The perfect tense, on the other hand, is often used of a completed action or an action that happened once.

agricola mercātōrem **pulsāvit**.   Pompēiānī agricolam
                                                         laudāvērunt.
The farmer punched the merchant.   *The Pompeians praised the*
                                                         farmer.

This well-preserved bar at Herculaneum gives us a good impression of the taberna where Clemens met Felix.

Practicing the Language

A When you have read the following story, answer the questions on the following page.

avārus

duo fūrēs ōlim ad vīllam contendēbant. in vīllā mercātor habitābat. mercātor erat senex et avārus. avārus multam pecūniam habēbat. fūrēs, postquam vīllam intrāvērunt, ātrium circumspectāvērunt.

"avārus," inquit fūr, "est sōlus. avārus servum nōn habet." 5
tum fūrēs tablīnum intrāvērunt. avārus clāmāvit et ferōciter pugnāvit, sed fūrēs senem facile superāvērunt.

"ubi est pecūnia, senex?" rogāvit fūr.

"servus fidēlis pecūniam in cubiculō custōdit," inquit senex. 10

"tū servum fidēlem nōn habēs, quod avārus es," clāmāvit fūr. tum fūrēs cubiculum petīvērunt.

"pecūniam videō," inquit fūr. fūrēs cubiculum intrāvērunt, ubi pecūnia erat, et pecūniam intentē spectāvērunt. sed ēheu! ingēns serpēns in pecūniā iacēbat. fūrēs serpentem timēbant 15
et ē vīllā celeriter festīnāvērunt.

in vīllā avārus rīdēbat et serpentem laudābat.

"tū es bonus servus. numquam dormīs. pecūniam meam semper servās."

avārus	*miser*
duo	*two*
habitābat	*was living*
inquit	*said*
pugnāvit	*fought*
facile	*easily*
fidēlis	*faithful*
custōdit	*is guarding*
ingēns	*huge*
serpēns	*snake*
iacēbat	*was lying*
timēbant	*were afraid of, feared*
celeriter	*quickly*
numquam	*never*
servās	*look after*

ingēns serpēns.

Questions

1 Who was hurrying to the merchant's house?
2 Write down three details about the merchant from lines 2–3.
3 What did the thieves do immediately after entering the house?
4 In line 5, why did one of the thieves think the merchant would be alone?
5 In line 6, the thieves found the merchant in his study. What do you think he was doing there?
6 In lines 6–7, which two Latin words tell you that the merchant resisted the thieves? Why did he lose the fight?
7 In line 9, who did the merchant say was guarding his money? Why did the thief think he was lying?
8 Which room did the thieves then enter? What did they see?
9 In lines 15–16, why did the thieves run away?
10 In lines 18–19, how did the merchant describe the **serpēns**? What reasons did he give?

B Write out each sentence completing it with the correct form of the noun from the parentheses. Then translate the Latin sentence. Translate carefully the tenses of the verb.

For example:　(servus, servī) in forō ambulābat.
　　　　　　　servus in forō ambulābat.
　　　　　　　The slave was walking in the forum.

　　　　　　　(amīcus, amīcī) forum intrāvērunt.
　　　　　　　amīcī forum intrāvērunt.
　　　　　　　The friends entered the forum.

1 (lībertus, lībertī) per viam festīnābat.
2 (servus, servī) pecūniam portābant.
3 (fūr, fūrēs) ātrium circumspectāvit.
4 (mercātor, mercātōrēs) clāmōrem audīvērunt.
5 (puer, puerī) fūrem superāvērunt.
6 (nauta, nautae) ad urbem festīnāvit.

C Turn back to the story, **Fēlīx et fūr**, on page 92. Read the lines 9–15 again, then make two lists, one for verbs in the imperfect tense, and one for verbs in the perfect. You should find five verbs in the imperfect, and seven verbs in the perfect tense. (The same verbs may occur more than once.)

Slaves and Freedmen

Wherever you traveled in the Roman world, you would find people who were slaves, like Grumio, Clemens, and Melissa. They belonged to a master or mistress to whom they had to give complete obedience. They were not free to make decisions for themselves. The Romans, like the other peoples who lived around the Mediterranean in classical times, regarded slavery as a normal and necessary part of life. Even those who realized that it was not a natural state of affairs made no serious attempt to abolish it. Slavery in the Roman Empire, however, was not based on racial prejudice. Slaves came from many different tribes and countries: Gaul, Germany, Britain, Spain, North Africa, Egypt, different parts of Greece and Asia Minor, Syria, and Palestine. Color itself did not signify slavery or obstruct advancement. Nor did slaves live separately from free people. Many slaves would live in the same house as their master. Slaves and free people could often be found working together.

People usually became slaves as a result either of being taken prisoner of war or of being captured by pirates; the children of slaves were automatically born into slavery. By the first century A.D., slaves made up 30 to 40 percent of the total population of Italy. A merchant like Caecilius would have had no fewer than a dozen in his house and many more working on his estates and in his businesses. Very wealthy men owned hundreds and sometimes even thousands of slaves. A man named Pedanius Secundus, who lived in Rome, kept four hundred in his house there. When one of them murdered him, they were all, in accordance with Roman law, put to death in spite of protests by the people of Rome.

Many people became slaves when captured in Rome's numerous wars. The scene above shows captives after a battle, sitting among the captured weapons and waiting to be sold. Families would be split up, and slaves would be given new names by their masters.

The Work and Treatment of Slaves

Slaves were employed in all kinds of work. Slaves might be owned by private individuals; a family's slaves were considered part of the **familia**. Publicly owned slaves carried out such municipal duties as bath and aqueduct maintenance. In the country, the life of slaves was rougher and harsher than in the cities. They worked as laborers on farms, as shepherds and ranchers on the big estates in southern Italy, in the mines, and on the building of roads and bridges. Some of the strongest slaves were bought for training as gladiators.

In the towns, slaves were used for both unskilled and skilled work. They were cooks and gardeners, general servants, hairdressers, laborers in factories, musicians, actors, and entertainers. Many received training that made them valuable as skilled accountants, secretaries, teachers, doctors, midwives, managers of businesses, managers of corporations like brickyards and warehousing, and managers of farms, vineyards, and orchards. In the course of doing such jobs, they were regularly in touch with their masters and other free men; they moved without restriction about the streets of the towns, went shopping, conducted business, visited temples, and attended shows at the theater and amphitheater. Foreign visitors to Rome and Italy were surprised that there was so little visible difference in dress, work, or treatment between a slave and a poor free man.

The law did not regard slaves as human beings, but as things that could be bought and sold, treated well or treated badly, according to the whim of their master. Common sense usually prevented a master from treating his slaves too harshly, since only fit, well-cared-for slaves were likely to work efficiently. A slave who was a skilled craftsman would be worth a large sum of money. A Roman master was generally too sensible to waste an expensive possession through carelessness. Although slaves were not protected by the law, there was one important exception: the law did not allow a master to kill a slave without just reason. The law said that slaves could not marry, nor could they own personal possessions. Yet, in actual practice, slaves could enter a marital relationship and could accumulate substantial sums of money.

Although many slaves did suffer personal degradation and inconsiderate or even cruel masters, many others were treated well. Frequently **vernae**, slaves born into the household, and **alumnī**, those acquired as babies or small children, were treated like members of the family. Slaves played with the children of the house as they grew up; under the supervision of the mother, they looked after the babies and helped with the early education of the younger children. A Roman might select a Greek nurse for his children so that they might learn Greek naturally. A young woman, on her marriage, often took her childhood nurse with her to her new home.

Slaves' jobs varied from serving drinks in the home and nursing children, to heavy labor, such as transporting goods.

Some were trained as gladiators.

Freeing a Slave

Not all slaves remained in slavery until they died. Compared to the other peoples in the Mediterranean area, the Romans were uniquely liberal in freeing slaves and in granting Roman citizenship. Freeing educated or trained slaves seems to have become almost standard procedure. In fact, so common was the practice that Emperor Augustus passed a law forbidding the freeing of slaves before age thirty. Freedom was sometimes given as a reward for particularly good service, sometimes as a sign of friendship and respect. A slave was permitted to own property, usually money (**peculium**), and could purchase his own freedom and that of another slave, frequently a spouse. Freedom was also very commonly given at the master's death by a statement in the will. The Augustan law also restricted this practice: not more than a hundred slaves (fewer in a small household) could be so freed.

The act of freeing a slave was called **manūmissiō**, a word connected with **manus** (hand) and **mittō** (send), meaning "a sending out from the hand" or "a setting free from control." Manumission was performed in several ways. The oldest method took the form of a legal ceremony before a public official, such as a judge. This is the ceremony seen in the picture at the beginning of this Stage. A witness claimed that the slave did not really belong to the master at all; the master did not deny the claim; the slave's head was then touched with a rod, and he was declared officially free. There were other simpler methods. A master might manumit a slave by a declaration in the presence of friends at home or merely by an invitation to recline on the couch at dinner.

Freedmen and Freedwomen

The ex-slave became a **lībertus** (freedman) or **līberta** (freedwoman). A freedwoman had fewer opportunities than a freedman. Often a freedwoman would marry her former master or a former slave. A freedman, however, had the opportunity to make his own way in life and even to become an important member of his community. Nevertheless he did not receive all the privileges of a citizen who had been born free. He could not stand as a candidate in public elections, nor could he become a high-ranking officer in the army. He still had obligations to his former master and had to work for him a fixed number of days each year. He would become a **cliēns**, one of the clients, and would visit his **patrōnus**, patron, regularly to pay his respects, usually early in the morning. He would be expected to help and support his former master whenever he could. This connection between them is seen very clearly in the names taken by a freedman. Suppose that his slave name had been Felix and his master had been Lucius Caecilius Iucundus. As soon as he was freed, Felix would take some of the names of his former master and call himself Lucius Caecilius Felix. Although a freedman had some restrictions, his children would enjoy all the privileges of full Roman citizenship.

Some freedmen continued to do the same work that they had previously done as slaves, while others were set up in business by their former masters. Some became priests in the temples or servants of the town council; the council secretaries, messengers, town clerk, and town crier were probably all freedmen. Some became very rich and powerful. Two freedmen at Pompeii, who were called the Vettii and who may have been brothers, owned a house which is one of the most magnificent in the town. The colorful paintings on its walls and the elegant marble fountains in the garden show clearly how prosperous the Vettii were. Another Pompeian freedman was the architect who designed the large theater; another was the father of Lucius Caecilius Iucundus.

Word Study

A Give the Latin word from which these words are derived:

1 furtive
2 intentional
3 pulsate
4 avarice
5 vituperative
6 fortitude
7 insuperable
8 redeem
9 bonanza
10 ferocious

B Write derivatives from **scrībit** which fit the following definitions:

1 To write in an aimless fashion.
2 Holy writing.
3 Writing on a tombstone or similar memorial.
4 A contract to receive a certain number of magazine issues.
5 A written drug recipe.
6 A copy, especially of an academic record.
7 A note written afterwards.

Atrium of the House of the Menander.

Stage 6
Vocabulary Checklist

abest	*is out, is absent*
aberat	*was out, was absent*
avārus	*miser*
bonus	*good*
emit	*buys*
erat	*was*
ferōciter	*fiercely*
festīnat	*hurries*
fortis	*brave, strong*
fūr: fūrem	*thief*
īnfāns: īnfantem	*baby, child*
intentē	*intently*
lībertus	*freedman, ex-slave*
ōlim	*once, some time ago*
parvus	*small, little*
per	*through*
postquam	*after, when*
pulsat	*hits, punches, whacks*
quod	*because*
rēs	*thing*
scrībit	*writes*
subitō	*suddenly*
superat	*overcomes, overpowers*
tum	*then*
tuus	*your, yours*
vituperat	*finds fault with, tells off, curses*

The two freedmen called the Vettii had their best dining room decorated with tiny pictures of cupids, seen here racing in chariots drawn by deer.

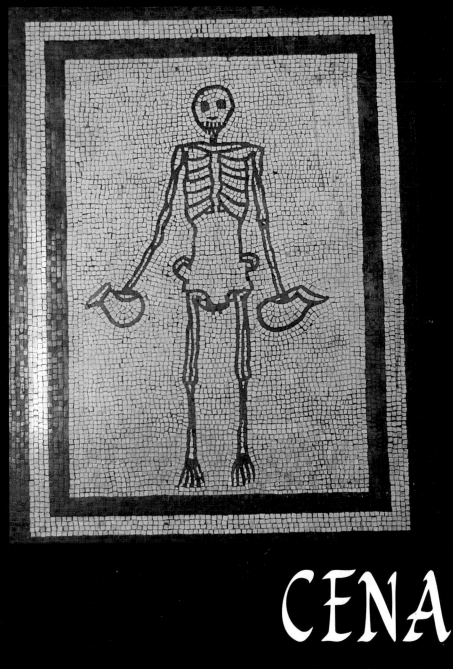

CENA

Stage 7

1 amīcus Caecilium vīsitābat.
  vīllam intrāvit.

2 Caecilius amīcum exspectābat.
  amīcum salūtāvit.

3 amīcus cum Caeciliō cēnābat.
  cēnam laudāvit.

4 amīcus pōculum īnspexit.
  vīnum gustāvit.

5 amīcus pōculum hausit.
  tum fābulam nārrāvit.

6 Caecilius plausit.
  "euge!" dīxit.

7 amīcī optimum vīnum
bibērunt.
tandem surrēxērunt.

8 servī in ātriō stābant.
iānuam aperuērunt.

9 Caecilius et amīcus
"valē" dīxērunt.
amīcus ē vīllā discessit.

fābula mīrābilis

multī amīcī cum Caeciliō cēnābant. Fēlīx quoque aderat. omnēs amīcī coquum laudāvērunt, quod cēna erat optima.

postquam omnēs cēnāvērunt, Caecilius clāmāvit, "ubi est Decēns? Decēns nōn adest." tum Caecilius Clēmentem ē vīllā mīsit. servus Decentem per urbem quaesīvit. 5

postquam servus ē vīllā discessit, Fēlīx pōculum hausit. tum lībertus fābulam mīrābilem nārrāvit:

"ōlim amīcus meus ex urbe discēdēbat. nox erat, sed lūna plēna lūcēbat. amīcus per viam festīnābat, ubi silva erat, et subitō centuriōnem cōnspexit. amīcus meus centuriōnem salūtāvit. 10 centuriō tamen nihil dīxit. tum centuriō tunicam dēposuit. ecce! centuriō ēvānuit. ingēns lupus subitō appāruit. amīcus meus valdē timēbat. ingēns lupus ululāvit et ad silvam festīnāvit. tunica in viā iacēbat. amīcus tunicam cautē īnspexit. ecce! tunica erat lapidea. tum amīcus rem intellēxit. ille centuriō erat versipellis." 15

fābula	*story*
mīrābilis	*marvelous, strange*
mīsit	*sent*
discessit	*departed, left*
pōculum	*wine-cup*
hausit	*drained*
ex urbe	*from the city*
nox	*night*
lūna	*moon*
plēna	*full*
lūcēbat	*was shining*
silva	*woods, forest*
centuriōnem	*centurion*
cōnspexit	*caught sight of*
dīxit	*said*
dēposuit	*took off*
ēvānuit	*vanished*
lupus	*wolf*
appāruit	*appeared*
ululāvit	*howled*
cautē	*cautiously*
īnspexit	*looked at, examined*
lapidea	*made of stone*
rem intellēxit	*understood the truth*
ille	*that*
versipellis	*werewolf*

About the Language I

A Study the following example:

> mercātor Caecilium vīsitābat. mercātor vīllam intrāvit.
> *A merchant was visiting Caecilius. The merchant entered the house.*

B In Stage 7, you have met a shorter way of saying this:

> mercātor Caecilium vīsitābat. vīllam intrāvit.
> *A merchant was visiting Caecilius. He entered the house.*

The following sentences behave in the same way:

> amīcī cum Caeciliō cēnābant. coquum laudāvērunt.
> *Friends were dining with Caecilius. They praised the cook.*

> ancilla in ātriō stābat. dominum salūtāvit.
> *The slave-girl was standing in the hall. She greeted the master.*

C Notice that Latin does not have to include a separate word for *he*, *she*, or *they*. **intrāvit** can mean *he entered* or *she entered*, depending on the context.

D Further examples:
1 Grumiō in culīnā labōrābat. cēnam parābat.
2 āctōrēs in theātrō clāmābant. fābulam agēbant.
3 Metella nōn erat in vīllā. in hortō ambulābat.
4 lībertī in tabernā bibēbant. Grumiōnem salūtāvērunt.
5 iuvenis pōculum hausit. vīnum laudāvit.

Symbolic of man's fate, this mosaic table-top comes from a summer triclinium.

Decēns

postquam Fēlīx fābulam nārrāvit, Caecilius et hospitēs plausērunt. tum omnēs tacēbant et aliam fābulam exspectābant. subitō clāmōrem audīvērunt. omnēs ad ātrium festīnāvērunt, ubi Clēmēns stābat.

Caecilius:	hercle! quid est? cūr tū clāmōrem facis?
Clēmēns:	Decēns, Decēns …
Caecilius:	quid est?
Clēmēns:	Decēns est mortuus.
omnēs:	quid? mortuus? ēheu!
	(*duo servī intrant.*)
Caecilius:	quid dīcis?
servus prīmus:	dominus meus ad vīllam tuam veniēbat; dominus gladiātōrem prope amphitheātrum cōnspexit.
servus secundus:	gladiātor dominum terruit, quod gladium ingentem vibrābat. tum gladiātor clāmāvit, "tū mē nōn terrēs, leō, tū mē nōn terrēs! leōnēs amīcum meum in arēnā necāvērunt, sed tū mē nōn terrēs!"
servus prīmus:	Decēns valdē timēbat."tū es īnsānus," inquit dominus. "ego nōn sum leō. sum homō."
servus secundus:	gladiātor tamen dominum ferōciter petīvit et eum ad amphitheātrum trāxit. dominus perterritus clāmāvit. Clēmēns clāmōrem audīvit.
servus prīmus:	Clēmēns, quod fortis erat, amphitheātrum intrāvit. Decentem in arēnā cōnspexit. dominus meus erat mortuus.
Caecilius:	ego rem intellegō! gladiātor erat Pugnāx. Pugnāx erat gladiātor nōtissimus. Pugnāx ōlim in arēnā pugnābat, et leō Pugnācem necāvit. Pugnāx nōn vīvit: Pugnāx est umbra. umbra Decentem necāvit.

hospitēs	guests
plausērunt	applauded
tacēbant	were silent
aliam	another
hercle!	by Hercules!
mortuus	dead
prīmus	first
gladiātōrem	gladiator
prope amphitheātrum	near the amphitheater
secundus	second
terruit	frightened
gladium	sword
vibrābat	was brandishing, was waving
in arēnā	in the arena
īnsānus	insane, crazy
homō	man
eum	him
trāxit	dragged
nōtissimus	very well-known
vīvit	is alive
umbra	ghost

Decēns valdē timēbat.

The inside of the Pompeii amphitheater as it is today, looking northwest towards Vesuvius.

post cēnam

postquam Caecilius rem explicāvit, omnēs amīcī tacēbant. mox
amīcī "valē" dīxērunt et ē vīllā discessērunt. per viam timidē
prōcēdēbant. nūllae stēllae lūcēbant. nūlla lūna erat in caelō. amīcī
nihil audīvērunt, quod viae dēsertae erant. amīcī per urbem tacitē
prōcēdēbant, quod umbram timēbant.   5
    subitō fēlēs ululāvit. amīcī valdē timēbant. omnēs per urbem
perterritī ruērunt, quod dē vītā dēspērābant. clāmōrem mīrābilem
faciēbant. multī Pompēiānī erant sollicitī, quod clāmōrem
audīvērunt. Caecilius tamen clāmōrem nōn audīvit, quod in
cubiculō dormiēbat.   10

explicāvit	*explained*
valē	*good-bye*
timidē	*nervously*
prōcēdēbant	*were advancing, were proceeding*
nūllae stēllae	*no stars*
in caelō	*in the sky*
dēsertae	*deserted*
fēlēs	*cat*
ruērunt	*rushed*
dē vītā dēspērābant	*were despairing of their lives*
sollicitī	*worried, anxious*

About the Language II

A In Stage 6, you met examples of the perfect tense. They looked like this:

> senex ad tabernam **ambulāvit**. amīcī in urbe **dormīvērunt**.
> *The old man walked to the inn.* *The friends slept in the city.*

This is a very common way in which Latin forms the perfect tense.

B In Stage 7, you have met other forms of the perfect tense. Look at the following examples:

PRESENT	PERFECT	
	singular	*plural*
appāret	appāruit	appāruērunt
	s/he appeared	*they appeared*
dīcit	dīxit	dīxērunt
	s/he said	*they said*
discēdit	discessit	discessērunt
	s/he left	*they left*
facit	fēcit	fēcērunt
	s/he made	*they made*
capit	cēpit	cēpērunt
	s/he took	*they took*
venit	vēnit	vēnērunt
	s/he came	*they came*

C Compare this with the way some words behave in English:

I send	I sent	I give	I gave	I read	I read
I run	I ran	I come	I came		

D If you are not sure whether a particular verb is in the present tense or the perfect tense, you can check by looking it up in the Complete Vocabulary section in the back of the book. Also, beginning with the Vocabulary Checklist for this Stage, verbs will be presented in two forms: the present tense, 3rd person singular, and then the perfect tense, 3rd person singular, followed by the meaning for the present tense form.

Practicing the Language

A Complete each sentence with the correct phrase, and then translate the sentence.

> For example: amīcī (vīllam intrāvit, cēnam laudāvērunt).
> amīcī **cēnam laudāvērunt**.
> *The friends praised the dinner.*

1 mercātor (ē vīllā discessit, clāmōrem audīvērunt).
2 ancillae (ad vīllam ambulāvit, in vīllā dormīvērunt).
3 leōnēs (gladiātōrem terruit, gladiātōrem cōnspexērunt).
4 lībertī (lūnam spectāvit, ad portum festīnāvērunt).
5 centuriō (fābulam audīvit, servum laudāvērunt).
6 fūr (per urbem ruit, centuriōnem terruērunt).
7 Caecilius et amīcus (leōnem cōnspexit, portum petīvērunt).

B Complete each sentence with the correct word. Then translate the sentence.

> For example: coquus (cēna, cēnam) parāvit.
> coquus **cēnam** parāvit.
> *The cook prepared the dinner.*
>
> (servus, servī) ad silvam ambulāvērunt.
> **servī** ad silvam ambulāvērunt.
> *The slaves walked to the wood.*

1 Clēmēns (dominus, dominum) excitāvit.
2 (lībertus, lībertum) fābulam nārrāvit.
3 (agricola, agricolae) ad forum festīnāvērunt.
4 ancilla (iānua, iānuam) aperuit.
5 (puella, puellae) clāmōrem fēcit.
6 (spectātor, spectātōrēs) cibum ad theātrum portāvērunt.
7 (senex, senēs) ē vīllā discessit.

C List the following verbs in two columns following the example. Translate each verb.

PRESENT		PERFECT	
portat	*s/he carries*	portāvit	*s/he carried*

coxit, vituperant, terruit, dūxit, coquit, faciunt, vituperāvērunt, audit, cēpit, terret, labōrāvērunt, audīvit, dūcit, fēcērunt, labōrant, capit

animal ferōx

postrīdiē, Fēlīx ad tablīnum vēnit. Caecilius eum ad vēnātiōnem invītāvit.

"ingēns aper," inquit Caecilius, "in monte Vesuviō latet. amīcī meī hunc aprum saepe vīdērunt. animal tamen est ferōx. amīcī eum numquam cēpērunt."

"ego vēnātor fortissimus sum," respondit Fēlīx. "gladiātōrem mortuum fortasse timeō. aper vīvus tamen mē nōn terret! sed cūr tū Quīntum ad vēnātiōnem nōn invītās? num Quīntus aprum timet?"

Caecilius igitur fīlium vocāvit. Quīntus laetissimus vēnābulum longum cēpit et cum patre et lībertō ad vēnātiōnem contendit. multī servī et multī canēs aderant. omnēs ad montem prōcessērunt, ubi aper latēbat.

servī, postquam aprum cōnspexērunt, clāmōrem fēcērunt. aper ferōx, quod clāmōrem audīvit, impetum fēcit. Fēlīx vēnābulum ēmīsit, sed aprum nōn percussit. lībertus, quod ad terram dēcidit, clāmāvit, "ēheu! aper mē petit!"

Quīntus fortiter prōcessit et vēnābulum suum ēmīsit. ecce! aprum trānsfīxit. ingēns aper ad terram mortuus dēcidit.

"euge!" clāmāvit Caecilius. "ōlim Fēlīx Quīntum servāvit. nunc fīlius meus Fēlīcem servāvit!"

animal	*animal*
ferōx	*fierce, ferocious*
postrīdīe	*the next day*
vēnit	*came*
vēnātiōnem	*hunt*
aper	*boar*
in monte Vesuviō	*on Mount Vesuvius*
latet	*lies hidden*
vīdērunt	*have seen*
numquam	*never*
cēpērunt	*(have) captured, caught*
vēnātor	*hunter*
fortissimus	*very brave*
fortasse	*perhaps*
vīvus	*live, living*
num Quīntus ... timet?	*Surely Quintus is not afraid?*
vēnābulum	*hunting spear*
longum	*long*
cēpit	*took*
prōcessērunt	*proceeded, advanced*
impetum	*attack, charge*
ēmīsit	*threw, hurled*
percussit	*hit, struck*
terram	*ground*
dēcidit	*fell down*
fortiter	*bravely*
prōcessit	*stepped forward*
suum	*his*
trānsfīxit	*pierced, stabbed*

Metella et Melissa

Metella, postquam Caecilius et Quīntus et Fēlīx ad vēnātiōnem
prōcessērunt, Melissam in vīllā quaerēbat. Metella culīnam
intrāvit, ubi Grumiō labōrābat. Grumiō erat īrātus.

"cūr tū es īrātus, Grumiō? cūr ferōciter circumspectās?" rogāvit
Metella.   5

"heri Melissa cēnam optimam parāvit," respondit coquus.
"hodiē ego cēnam pessimam parō, quod nūllus cibus adest. heri
multus cibus erat in culīnā. ancilla omnem cibum coxit. Melissa est
pulcherrima sed Melissa est pestis!"

Metella ē culīnā discessit et ad tablīnum festīnāvit, ubi Clēmēns   10
labōrābat. Clēmēns quoque erat īrātus.

"Melissa est pulcherrima sed Melissa est pestis!" clāmāvit
servus.

"quid fēcit Melissa?" rogāvit Metella.

"heri Melissa in tablīnō labōrābat," respondit Clēmēns. "hodiē   15
ego in tablīnō labōrō. ecce! cērae et stilī absunt. nihil est in locō
propriō."

Metella, postquam ē tablīnō discessit, hortum intrāvit. Metella
Melissam in hortō vīdit. ēheu! ancilla lacrimābat.

"Melissa, cūr lacrimās?" rogāvit Metella.   20

"lacrimō quod Grumiō et Clēmēns mē vituperant," respondit
ancilla.

"ego tamen tē nōn vituperō," inquit Metella. "ego tē laudō. ecce!
tū crīnēs meōs optimē compōnis. stolam meam optimē compōnis.
fortasse Grumiō et Clēmēns tē nōn laudant; sed ego tē laudō, quod   25
mē dīligenter cūrās."

heri	yesterday
pessimam	very bad
coxit	cooked
pulcherrima	very beautiful
fēcit	has done
stilī	pens
in locō propriō	in the right place
vīdit	saw
crīnēs	hair
optimē	very well
compōnis	arrange
stolam	(long) dress
dīligenter	carefully
cūrās	take care of

Roman Beliefs about Life after Death

The Romans did not place the tombs of the dead in quiet, lonely places but by the side of roads just outside towns, where they could be seen and admired. The tombs at Pompeii can still be seen along the roads that go north from the Herculaneum Gate and south from the Nuceria Gate.

Some were grand and impressive and looked like small houses; others were plain and simple. Inside a tomb there was a chest or vase containing the ashes of the dead person; sometimes there were recesses in the walls of a tomb to hold the remains of several members of a family. The ashes of poor people, who could not afford the expense of a tomb, were buried more simply. At this time cremation was the normal way of disposing of the dead.

In building their cemeteries along busy roads rather than in peaceful and secluded places, the Romans were not showing any lack of respect. On the contrary, they believed that, unless the dead were properly treated, their ghosts would haunt the living and possibly do them harm. It was most important to provide the dead with a tomb or grave, where their ghosts could have a home. But it was also thought that they would want to be close to the life of the living. One tomb has this inscription: "I see and gaze upon all who come to and from the city" and another, "Lollius has been placed by the side of the road in order that everyone who passes may say to him 'Hello, Lollius'."

Tombs outside the Herculaneum Gate.

It was believed that the dead in some way continued the activities of life and therefore had to be supplied with the things they would need. A craftsman would want his tools, a woman her jewelry, children their toys. When the bodies of the dead were cremated, certain of their possessions were burned or buried with them. A Greek writer called Lucian tells the story of a husband who had burned all his dead wife's jewelry and clothes on the funeral pyre so that she might have them in the next world. A week later he was trying to comfort himself by reading a book about life after death, when the ghost of his wife appeared. She began to reproach him because he had not burned one of her gilded sandals, which, she said, was lying under a chest. The family dog then barked, and the ghost disappeared. The husband looked under the chest, found the sandal, and burned it. The ghost was now content and did not appear again.

The ghosts of the dead were also thought to be hungry and thirsty and therefore had to be given food and drink. Offerings of eggs, beans, lentils, flour and wine were placed regularly at the tomb. Sometimes holes were made in the tomb so that food and wine could be poured inside. Wine was a convenient substitute for blood, the favorite drink of the dead. At the funeral and on special occasions, animals were sacrificed, and their blood was offered.

Inside a Pompeian tomb, with recesses for the ashes.

Section through a Roman burial in Caerleon, Wales. A pipe ran down into the container for the ashes, so that gifts of food and drink could be poured in.

Cremation urns

Ashes were buried in containers of many materials, including stone, metal and glass. One wealthy Pompeian had his ashes buried in this fabulously expensive, hand-carved blue and white glass vase, which was found in one of the tombs outside the Herculaneum Gate. Poor people might put the ashes of the dead in second-hand storage jars which were then buried in the earth.

It was thought, however, that in spite of these attempts to care for them, the dead did not lead a very happy existence. In order to help them forget their unhappiness, their tombs were often decorated with garlands of flowers and surrounded by little gardens, a custom which has lasted to this day, although its original meaning has changed. With the same purpose in mind, the family and friends of a dead person held a banquet after the funeral and on the anniversary of the death. Sometimes these banquets took place in a dining room attached to the tomb itself, sometimes in the family home. The ghosts of the dead were thought to attend and enjoy these cheerful occasions.

In addition to these ceremonies, two festivals for the dead were held every year. At one of these, families remembered parents and relations who had died; at the other, they performed rites to exorcise any ghosts in their houses who might be lonely or hungry and therefore dangerous.

Some people also believed in the Greek myths about the underworld, where the good lived happily forever in the Elysian Fields and where the wicked were punished for their crimes in Tartarus. Stories were told about the punishments suffered by famous evildoers such as the wicked Tityus, who had his liver pecked out by vultures, and the daughters of Danaus, who were condemned to carry water forever in pots with holes in the bottom. By the first century A.D., most Romans did not take these stories literally, although they continued to incorporate them into their art and literature.

An open-air dining room attached to a tomb outside the Herculaneum Gate, where the relatives could feast with the dead.

There were a few people who did not believe in any form of life after death. These were the followers of a Greek philosopher called Epicurus who taught that, when a man died, the breath that gave him life dissolved in the air and was lost forever. The Epicureans, therefore, could devote all their energy to making the most of life in this world.

Most Romans, however, felt no need to question their traditional beliefs and customs which kept the dead alive in their memories and tried to ensure that the spirits were happy and at peace.

A bronze head of Epicurus, from a villa at Herculaneum.

Word Study

A Match the word in Column II that comes closest in meaning to the words in Column I:

I	II
lachrymose	nearness
pulchritude	silent
tacit	beauty
internecine	tearful
propinquity	deadly

B What do the following derivatives of **facit** mean?

1 facsimile
2 manufacture
3 perfect
4 mollify
5 beneficial

What do the following derivatives of **omnis** mean?

1 omnibus
2 omnipotent
3 omniscient
4 omnivorous

C Fill in the blanks with derivatives from the following Latin words:

cōnspicit   nihil   terret
mortuus   rogat

1 The costume made the actor very . . . . . .
2 Our team intends to . . . . . the opposition.
3 He had to submit to a thorough police . . . . . .
4 The president was . . . . . by the absence of the main speaker for the evening.
5 The Halloween costume struck . . . . . into the small children.

Stage 7
Vocabulary Checklist

cēnat: cēnāvit	*eats dinner, dines*
centuriō	*centurion*
cōnspicit: cōnspexit	*catches sight of*
cum	*with*
facit: fēcit	*makes, does*
heri	*yesterday*
ingēns: ingentem	*huge*
intellegit: intellēxit	*understands*
lacrimat: lacrimāvit	*cries, weeps*
mortuus	*dead*
nārrat: nārrāvit	*tells, relates*
necat: necāvit	*kills*
nihil	*nothing*
omnis	*all*
parat: parāvit	*prepares*
pestis: pestem	*pest, rascal*
pōculum	*cup (often for wine)*
prōcēdit: prōcessit	*advances, proceeds*
prope	*near*
pulcher: pulchrum	*beautiful, handsome*
rogat: rogāvit	*asks*
tacitē	*quietly, silently*
tamen	*however*
terret: terruit	*frightens*
umbra	*ghost, shadow*
valdē	*very much, very*

Dead sinners being punished in the underworld: Sisyphus had to roll a stone forever; Ixion was tied to a revolving wheel; and Tantalus was never able to quench his thirst.

GLADIATORES

1 nūntiī spectāculum
nūntiābant.
Pompēiānī nūntiōs audiēbant.

2 gladiātōrēs per viam
prōcēdēbant.
Pompēiānī gladiātōrēs
laudābant.

3 puellae iuvenēs salūtāvērunt.
iuvenēs quoque ad
amphitheātrum
contendēbant.

4 servī fēminās spectābant,
quod fēminae ad
spectāculum contendēbant.

5 puerī per viam festīnābant.
puellae puerōs salūtāvērunt.

6 Pompēiānī tabernās nōn
intrābant, quod tabernae
erant clausae.

amphitheātrum

7 postquam gladiātōrēs
Pompēiānōs salūtāvērunt,
Pompēiānī plausērunt.

8 Pompēiānī gladiātōrēs intentē
spectābant, quod gladiātōrēs
in arēnā pugnābant.

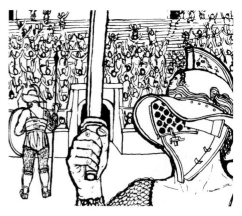

9 spectātōrēs murmillōnēs
incitābant, quod murmillōnēs
saepe victōrēs erant.

gladiātōrēs

Rēgulus erat senātor Rōmānus. in vīllā magnificā habitābat. vīlla erat prope Nūceriam. Nūcerīnī et Pompēiānī erant inimīcī. Nūcerīnī, quod amphitheātrum nōn habēbant, saepe ad amphitheātrum Pompēiānum veniēbant; saepe erant turbulentī.

Rēgulus ōlim spectāculum splendidum in amphitheātrō ēdidit, 5 quod diem nātālem celebrābat. multī Nūcerīnī igitur ad urbem vēnērunt. cīvēs Pompēiānī erant īrātī, quod Nūcerīnī viās complēbant. omnēs tamen ad forum contendērunt, ubi nūntiī stābant. nūntiī spectāculum optimum nūntiābant:

"gladiātōrēs adsunt! vīgintī gladiātōrēs hodiē pugnant! rētiāriī 10 adsunt! murmillōnēs adsunt! bēstiāriī bēstiās ferōcēs agitant!"

Nūcerīnī, postquam nūntiōs audīvērunt, ad amphitheātrum quam celerrimē contendērunt. Pompēiānī quoque ad amphitheātrum festīnāvērunt. hī Pompēiānī Nūcerīnōs et Rēgulum vituperābant, quod Nūcerīnī erant turbulentī. omnēs 15 vehementer clāmābant. cīvēs, tamen, postquam amphitheātrum intrāvērunt, tacuērunt. prīmam pugnam exspectābant.

senātor Rōmānus	*Roman senator*
magnificā	*magnificent*
Nūceriam	*Nuceria (a town near Pompeii)*
Nūcerīnī	*the people of Nuceria*
inimīcī	*enemies*
saepe	*often*
turbulentī	*rowdy, disorderly*
spectāculum	*show, spectacle*
splendidum	*splendid*
ēdidit	*presented*
diem nātālem	*birthday*
celebrābat	*was celebrating*
cīvēs	*citizens*
complēbant	*were filling*
nūntiābant	*were announcing*
vīgintī	*twenty*
rētiāriī	*retiarii, net-fighters*
murmillōnēs	*murmillones, heavily armed gladiators*
bēstiāriī	*beast-fighters*
bēstiās	*wild animals, beasts*
quam celerrimē	*as quickly as possible*
hī	*these*
vehementer	*loudly, violently*
tacuērunt	*fell silent*

The amphitheater at Pompeii. Notice one of the staircases that led up to the top seats. The public sports ground is behind the trees on the right. On performance days, the open space would have been full of stalls selling refreshments and souvenirs.

A retiarius with his trident, net, and protection for his right arm and neck.

in arēnā

duo rētiāriī et duo murmillōnēs arēnam intrāvērunt. postquam gladiātōrēs spectātōrēs salūtāvērunt, tuba sonuit. tum gladiātōrēs pugnam commīsērunt. murmillōnēs Pompēiānōs valdē dēlectābant, quod saepe victōrēs erant. Pompēiānī igitur murmillōnēs incitābant. sed rētiāriī, quod erant expedītī, 5 murmillōnēs facile ēvītāvērunt.

"rētiāriī nōn pugnant! rētiāriī sunt ignāvī!" clāmāvērunt Pompēiānī. Nūcerīnī tamen respondērunt, "rētiāriī sunt callidī! rētiāriī murmillōnēs dēcipiunt!"

murmillōnēs rētiāriōs frūstrā ad pugnam prōvocāvērunt. tum 10 murmillō clāmāvit, "ūnus murmillō facile duōs rētiāriōs superat."

Pompēiānī plausērunt. tum murmillō rētiāriōs statim petīvit. murmillō et rētiāriī ferōciter pugnāvērunt. rētiāriī tandem murmillōnem graviter vulnerāvērunt. tum rētiāriī alterum murmillōnem petīvērunt. hic murmillō fortiter pugnāvit, sed 15 rētiāriī eum quoque superāvērunt.

Pompēiānī, quod īrātī erant, murmillōnēs vituperābant; missiōnem tamen postulābant, quod murmillōnēs fortēs erant. Nūcerīnī mortem postulābant. omnēs spectātōrēs tacēbant et Rēgulum intentē spectābant. Rēgulus, quod Nūcerīnī mortem 20 postulābant, pollicem vertit. Pompēiānī erant īrātī, et vehementer clāmābant. rētiāriī tamen, postquam Rēgulus signum dedit, murmillōnēs interfēcērunt.

tuba	trumpet	ūnus	one
sonuit	sounded	graviter	seriously
pugnam commīsērunt	began the fight	vulnerāvērunt	wounded
		alterum	the second, the other
victōrēs	victors, winners		
expedītī	lightly armed	hic	this
ēvītāvērunt	avoided	missiōnem	release
ignāvī	cowards	mortem	death
callidī	clever, smart	pollicem vertit	turned his thumb up
dēcipiunt	are deceiving, are tricking		
		dedit	gave
frūstrā	in vain	interfēcērunt	killed
prōvocāvērunt	challenged		

vēnātiō

When you have read this story, answer the questions opposite.

postquam rētiāriī ex arēnā discessērunt, tuba iterum sonuit. subitō
multī cervī arēnam intrāvērunt. cervī per tōtam arēnam currēbant,
quod perterritī erant. tum canēs ferōcēs per portam intrāvērunt.
canēs statim cervōs perterritōs agitāvērunt et interfēcērunt.
postquam canēs cervōs superāvērunt, lupī arēnam intrāvērunt.   5
lupī, quod valdē ēsuriēbant, canēs ferōciter petīvērunt. canēs erant
fortissimī, sed lupī facile canēs superāvērunt.

  Nūcerīnī erant laetissimī et Rēgulum laudābant. Pompēiānī
tamen nōn erant contentī, sed clāmābant, "ubi sunt leōnēs? cūr
Rēgulus leōnēs retinet?"   10

  Rēgulus, postquam hunc clāmōrem audīvit, signum dedit.
statim trēs leōnēs per portam ruērunt. tuba iterum sonuit. bēstiāriī
arēnam audācissimē intrāvērunt. leōnēs tamen bēstiāriōs nōn
petīvērunt. leōnēs in arēnā recubuērunt. leōnēs obdormīvērunt!

  tum Pompēiānī erant īrātissimī, quod Rēgulus spectāculum   15
rīdiculum ēdēbat. Pompēiānī Rēgulum et Nūcerīnōs ex
amphitheātrō agitāvērunt. Nūcerīnī per viās fugiēbant, quod
valdē timēbant. Pompēiānī tamen gladiōs suōs dēstrīnxērunt et
multōs Nūcerīnōs interfēcērunt. ecce! sanguis nōn in arēnā sed per
viās fluēbat.   20

iterum	*again*
cervī	*deer*
ēsuriēbant	*were hungry*
retinet	*is holding back*
hunc	*this*
trēs	*three*
audācissimē	*very boldly*
recubuērunt	*lay down*
obdormīvērunt	*went to sleep*
īrātissimī	*very angry*
rīdiculum	*ridiculous, silly*
ēdēbat	*was presenting*
fugiēbant	*began to run away, began to flee*
suōs	*their*
dēstrīnxērunt	*drew*

Questions

1 What two things happened after the retiarii left the arena?
2 How did the deer feel? What two things happened to them?
3 Why did the wolves chase the dogs? How did the chase end?
4 What were the different feelings of the Nucerians and Pompeians?
5 Why were the Pompeians feeling like this?
6 What two things happened after Regulus gave the signal?
7 What would the spectators have expected to happen? What went wrong?
8 Why were the Pompeians angry? What did they do?
9 What made the riot so serious?
10 Re-read the last sentence. Why do you think **ecce!** is put in front of it?

About the Language I

A From Stage 2 onwards, you have met sentences like these:

amīcus **puellam** salūtat.	*The friend greets **the girl**.*
dominus **servum** vituperābat.	*The master was cursing **the slave**.*
puerī **leōnem** spectāvērunt.	*The boys watched **the lion**.*

In each of these examples, the person who has something done to him or her is indicated in Latin by the **accusative singular**.

B In Stage 8, you have met sentences like these:

amīcus **puellās** salūtat.	*The friend greets **the girls**.*
dominus **servōs** vituperābat.	*The master was cursing **the slaves**.*
puerī **leōnēs** spectāvērunt.	*The boys watched **the lions**.*

In these examples, the persons who have something done to them are indicated in Latin by the **accusative plural**.

C You have now met the following cases:

	FIRST DECLENSION	SECOND DECLENSION	THIRD DECLENSION
SINGULAR			
nominative	puella	servus	mercātor
accusative	puellam	servum	mercātōrem
PLURAL			
nominative	puellae	servī	mercātōrēs
accusative	puellās	servōs	mercātōrēs

D Further examples:

1 agricola gladiātōrem laudāvit. agricola gladiātōrēs laudāvit.
2 servus agricolam interfēcit. servus agricolās interfēcit.
3 centuriō servōs laudāvit.
4 puer āctōrēs ad theātrum dūxit.
5 senex āctōrem ad forum dūxit.
6 amīcus fābulās nārrāvit.
7 amīcī ancillam salūtāvērunt.
8 agricolae nūntiōs audīvērunt.

pāstor et leō

ōlim pāstor in silvā ambulābat. subitō pāstor leōnem cōnspexit. leō
tamen pāstōrem nōn agitāvit. leō lacrimābat! pāstor, postquam
leōnem cōnspexit, erat attonitus et rogāvit,
    "cūr lacrimās, leō? cūr mē nōn agitās? cūr mē nōn cōnsūmis?"
    leō trīstis pedem ostendit. pāstor spīnam in pede cōnspexit, tum   *5*
clāmāvit,
    "ego spīnam videō! spīnam ingentem videō! nunc intellegō! tū
lacrimās, quod pēs dolet."
    pāstor, quod benignus et fortis erat, ad leōnem cautē vēnit et
spīnam īnspexit. leō fremuit, quod ignāvus erat.   *10*
    "leō!" exclāmāvit pāstor, "ego perterritus sum, quod tū fremis.
sed tē adiuvō. ecce! spīna!"
    postquam hoc dīxit, pāstor spīnam quam celerrimē extrāxit. leō
ignāvus iterum fremuit et ē silvā festīnāvit.
    posteā, Rōmānī hunc pāstōrem comprehendērunt, quod   *15*
Christiānus erat, et eum ad arēnam dūxērunt. postquam arēnam
intrāvit, pāstor spectātōrēs vīdit et valdē timēbat. tum pāstor
bēstiās vīdit et clāmāvit, "nunc mortuus sum! videō leōnēs et
lupōs. ēheu!"
    tum ingēns leō ad eum ruit. leō, postquam pāstōrem olfēcit, nōn   *20*
eum cōnsūmpsit sed lambēbat! pāstor attonitus leōnem agnōvit et
dīxit,
    "tē agnōscō! tū es leō trīstis! spīna erat in pede tuō."
    leō iterum fremuit, et pāstōrem ex arēnā ad salūtem dūxit.

attonitus	*astonished*	**hoc**	*this*
trīstis	*sad*	**extrāxit**	*pulled out*
pedem	*foot, paw*	**posteā**	*afterwards*
ostendit	*showed*	**comprehendērunt**	*arrested*
spīnam	*thorn*	**Christiānus**	*Christian*
dolet	*hurts*	**olfēcit**	*smelled, sniffed*
benignus	*kind*	**lambēbat**	*began to lick*
fremuit	*roared*	**agnōvit**	*recognised*
exclāmāvit	*shouted*	**ad salūtem**	*to safety*
adiuvō	*help*		

About the Language II

A Study the following pairs of sentences:

Pompēiānī erant īrātī.
The Pompeians were angry.

Pompēiānī erant **īrātissimī**.
The Pompeians were very angry.

gladiātor est nōtus.
The gladiator is famous.

gladiātor est **nōtissimus**.
The gladiator is very famous.

māter erat laeta.
The mother was happy.

māter erat **laetissima**.
The mother was very happy.

The words in bold type are known as **superlatives**. Notice how they are translated in the examples above.

B A few superlatives are formed in a different way:

mōns est pulcher.
The mountain is beautiful.

mōns Vesuvius est **pulcherrimus**.
Mount Vesuvius is very beautiful.

C Further examples:

1 mercātor est trīstis. senex est trīstissimus.
2 canis erat ferōx. leō erat ferōcissimus.
3 amīcus fābulam longissimam nārrāvit.
4 murmillōnēs erant fortēs, sed rētiāriī erant fortissimī.
5 Melissa erat pulcherrima.

A duel reaches its climax in this painting from a tomb at Pompeii.

Practicing the Language

A Complete each sentence with the correct word from the box.
Then translate the sentence.

> ego   leōnēs
> tū   vēndō
> amīcōs   spectās

1 ..... multās vīllās habeō.
2 ego servōs ......
3 tū gladiātōrēs ......

4 ego ..... salūtō.
5 ..... ancillās laudās.
6 tū ..... agitās.

B Complete each sentence with the right word from the parentheses. Then translate the sentence.

1 tū es vēnālīcius; tū servōs in forō (vēndō, vēndis, vēndit).
2 ego sum gladiātor; ego in arēnā (pugnō, pugnās, pugnat).
3 Fēlīx est lībertus; Fēlīx cum Caeciliō (cēnō, cēnās, cēnat).
4 ego multōs spectātōrēs in amphitheātrō (videō, vidēs, videt).
5 tū in vīllā magnificā (habitō, habitās, habitat).
6 Rēgulus hodiē diem nātālem (celebrō, celebrās, celebrat).
7 tū saepe ad amphitheātrum (veniō, venīs, venit).
8 ego rem (intellegō, intellegis, intellegit).

C The following words, in the accusative plural, occur in the accusative singular in the **pāstor et leō** story (page 131). Find the accusative singular forms in the story. Make a three-columned chart for first, second, and third declension, and list each singular and plural pair in the proper column.

> leōnēs   pāstōrēs
> spīnās   arēnās

Then find the accusative plural forms for the following singular nouns, and continue the chart:

> lupum
> bēstiam
> spectātōrem

Gladiator fights were often performed to the sound of trumpet and organ.

Gladiatorial Shows

Among the most popular entertainments in all parts of the Roman world were shows in which gladiators fought each other. These contests were usually held in an **amphitheātrum** (amphitheater). This was a large oval building, without a roof, in which rising tiers of seats surrounded an **arēna**. Canvas awnings, supported by ropes and pulleys, were spread over part of the seating area to give shelter from the sun. The amphitheater at Pompeii was large enough to contain the whole population as well as many visitors from nearby towns. Spectators paid no admission fee as the shows were given by wealthy individuals at their own expense.

Bird's-eye view of the amphitheater showing the awning. Compare the drawing on page 124. The building held around 20,000 people, and the number of seats was being increased when the city was destroyed.

Among the many advertisements for gladiatorial shows that are to be seen painted on the walls of buildings is this one:

> **Twenty pairs of gladiators, given by Lucretius Satrius Valens, priest of Nero, and ten pairs of gladiators provided by his son will fight at Pompeii from 8 to 12 April. There will also be an animal hunt. Awnings will be provided.**

Soon after dawn on the day of a show, the spectators would begin to take their places. A trumpet (**tuba**) blared and priests came out to perform the religious ceremony with which the games began. Then the gladiators entered in procession, paraded round the arena, and saluted the sponsor of the show. The gladiators were then paired off to fight each other, and the contests began.

The gladiators were slaves, condemned criminals, prisoners of war, or free volunteers; they lived and trained in a school or barracks under the supervision of a professional trainer.

Part of the program of one particular show, together with details of the results, reads as follows:

A Thracian versus a Murmillo
Won: Pugnax from Nero's school:
  3 times a winner
Died: Murranus from Nero's school:
  3 times a winner

A heavily armed gladiator versus a Thracian
Won: Cycnus from the school of Julius:
  8 times a winner
Allowed to live: Atticus from the school of Julius:
  14 times a winner

Chariot Fighters
Won: Scylax from the school of Julius:
  26 times a winner
Allowed to live: Publius Ostorius:
  51 times a winner

The fight ended with the death or surrender of one of the gladiators. The illustrations above, based on a relief from the tomb of a wealthy Pompeian, show the defeated gladiator appealing to the spectators; the victor stands by ready to kill him if they decide that he deserves to die. Notice the arm raised in appeal. The spectators indicated their wishes by turning their thumbs up or down: probably turning the thumb up towards the chest meant "kill him," while lowering the thumb to the closed fist meant "let him live." The final decision for death or mercy was made by the sponsor of the games. It was not unusual for the life of the loser to be spared, especially if he were a well-known gladiator with a good number of victories to his credit. The most successful gladiators were great favorites with the crowd and received gifts of money from their admirers. One popular Pompeian gladiator was described as **suspīrium puellārum**, "the girls' heartthrob." Eventually, if a gladiator survived long enough or showed great skill and courage, he would be awarded the wooden sword. This was a high honor and meant he would not have to fight again.

Gladiators' Armor

Gladiators were not all armed in the same way. Some, who were known as Samnites, carried an oblong shield and a short sword; others, known as Thracians, had a round shield and a curved sword or dagger. Another type of gladiator armed with sword and shield wore a helmet with a crest shaped like a fish; the Greek name for the fish was "mormillos" and the gladiator was known as a **murmillō**. The murmillones were often matched against the **rētiāriī** who were armed with **rētia** (nets) and three-pronged tridents.

Other types of gladiator fought with spears, on horseback, or from chariots. Occasionally women gladiators were used, bringing additional variety to the show.

A great deal of gladiators' armor was discovered at Pompeii with traces of fabrics embroidered with gold thread. The performers must have looked spectacular, like modern circus artists – except for the bloodshed. Here are two sorts of helmet, a retiarius' neck-guard, a greave (leg-protector) and a shield.

Animal Hunts

Many shows also offered a **vēnātiō**, a hunt of wild animals. The **bēstiae** (wild beasts) were released from cages into the arena, where they were hunted by specially trained beast-fighters called **bēstiāriī**. In the illustration below, you can see a wolf, hares, a wild boar, a bull, and a lion.

The hunters, who wore light clothing, relied only on a thrusting spear and their agility to avoid injury. By the end of the hunt, all the animals, and occasionally a few hunters, had been killed, and their bodies were dragged out from the sandy floor of the arena to be disposed of.

The Riot at Pompeii

The story told in this Stage is based on an actual event which occurred in A.D. 59. In addition to the evidence given in the wall-painting (*above*), the event is also described by the Roman historian Tacitus in these words:

> About this time, a slight incident led to a serious outburst of rioting between the people of Pompeii and Nuceria. It occurred at a show of gladiators, sponsored by Livineius Regulus. While hurling insults at each other, in the usual manner of country people, they suddenly began to throw stones as well. Finally, they drew swords and attacked each other. The men of Pompeii won the fight. As a result, most of the families of Nuceria lost a father or a son. Many of the wounded were taken to Rome, where the Emperor Nero requested the Senate to hold an inquiry. After the investigation, the Senate forbade the Pompeians to hold such shows for ten years. Livineius Regulus and others who had encouraged the riot were sent into exile.

This drawing of a gladiator with the palm of victory was scratched on a wall with a message that may refer to the riot and its aftermath. "Campanians, in your moment of victory you perished along with the Nucerians."

CAMPANI VICTORIAVNA
CVMNVCERINIS PERISTIS

Word Study

A Give the Latin word from which these words are derived:

1 gladiator
2 portal
3 Pennsylvania
4 agitator
5 incite
6 spectacle
7 renounce
8 inhabitant

B Match the derivative and its meaning:

1 facile   **a** to reason earnestly with someone
2 sanguine   **b** eager to fight, quarrelsome
3 totalitarian   **c** childish
4 pedestrian   **d** achieved with little difficulty
5 expostulate   **e** cheerfully optimistic
6 pugnacious   **f** to condemn openly; censure
7 puerile   **g** very ordinary, commonplace
8 denounce   **h** upheld by authoritarian means

C Give the derivatives of **dūcit** suggested in the phrases below.

1 To take an amount from the total: - -duce.
2 A ceremony taking new members into an organization: - -duct- - -.
3 Easily taking shape or easily molded: duct- - -.
4 The leader of an orchestra: - - -duct- -.
5 Taken away by a kidnapper: - -duct- -.
6 Applying in a specific case a conclusion taken from a generality: - -duct- - -.

Stage 8
Vocabulary Checklist

agitat: agitāvit	*chases, hunts*
cōnsūmit: cōnsūmpsit	*eats*
dūcit: dūxit	*leads*
eum	*him*
facile	*easily*
ferōx	*fierce, ferocious*
gladius	*sword*
habitat: habitāvit	*lives*
hic	*this*
ignāvus	*cowardly* (also *lazy* in other contexts)
incitat: incitāvit	*urges on, encourages*
nūntius	*messenger*
pēs: pedem	*foot, paw*
porta	*gate*
postulat: postulāvit	*demands*
puer: puerum	*boy*
pugnat: pugnāvit	*fights*
recumbit: recubuit	*lies down, reclines*
saepe	*often*
sanguis: sanguinem	*blood*
silva	*woods, forest*
spectāculum	*show, spectacle*
statim	*at once*
tōtus	*whole*

A retiarius who lost his fight. The symbol beside his trident is θ (theta), the first letter of the Greek word for death (thanatos).

THERMAE

Stage 9

1 Quīntus ad thermās vēnit.

2 Quīntus servō pecūniam dedit.

3 amīcī Quīntum laetē salūtāvērunt, quod diem nātālem celebrābat.

4 Quīntus discum novum ferēbat. Quīntus amīcīs discum ostendit.

5 postquam Quīntus discum ēmīsit, discus statuam percussit.

6 ēheu! statua nāsum frāctum habēbat.

7 Metella et Melissa in forō
  ambulābant. Metella fīliō
  dōnum quaerēbat.

8 fēminae mercātōrem
  cōnspexērunt. mercātor
  fēminīs togās ostendit.

9 Metella Quīntō togam ēlēgit.
  Melissa mercātōrī pecūniam
  dedit.

10 Grumiō cēnam optimam
in culīnā parābat. coquus
Quīntō cēnam parābat,
quod diem nātālem
celebrābat.

11 multī hospitēs cum
Quīntō cēnābant.
Clēmēns hospitibus
vīnum offerēbat.

12 ancilla triclīnium intrāvit.
Quīntus ancillae signum
dedit. ancilla suāviter
cantāvit.

thermae

cīvēs Pompēiānī trēs thermās habēbant. cīvēs cotīdiē ad thermās
ībant. servī post dominōs ambulābant. servī oleum et strigilēs
ferēbant.

    cīvēs et servī, postquam thermās intrāvērunt, āthlētās et pugilēs
vidēbant. āthlētae in palaestrā sē exercēbant. multī saliēbant, multī   5
discōs ēmittēbant. servī cīvibus discōs quaerēbant. servī,
postquam discōs invēnērunt, ad cīvēs reveniēbant. tum servī
cīvibus discōs trādēbant.

    cīvēs, postquam sē exercuērunt, apodytērium intrābant. omnēs
in apodytēriō togās dēpōnēbant, et tepidārium intrābant. cīvēs in   10
tepidāriō paulīsper sedēbant, tum ad caldārium ībant. in caldāriō
erant multae sellae. ibi dominī sedēbant et garriēbant. servī
dominīs oleum et strigilēs ferēbant. servī dominōs dīligenter
rādēbant. thermae Pompēiānōs valdē dēlectābant.

thermae	*baths*
ībant	*used to go*
oleum	*oil*
strigilēs	*strigils, scrapers*
ferēbant	*used to carry*
āthlētās	*athletes*
pugilēs	*boxers*
in palaestrā	*in the palaestra*
sē exercēbant	*were exercising*
discōs ēmittēbant	*were throwing discuses, were throwing the discus*
invēnērunt	*found*
apodytērium	*changing room*
togās	*togas*
tepidārium	*warm room*
paulīsper	*for a short time*
caldārium	*hot room*
ibi	*there*
garriēbant	*gossiped*
rādēbant	*scraped*

Strigils and oil pots.

in palaestrā

Caecilius Quīntō discum dedit, quod diem nātālem celebrābat.
tum Caecilius fīlium ad thermās dūxit, ubi palaestra erat. servus
Quīntō discum ferēbat.

Caecilius et fīlius, postquam thermās intrāvērunt, ad
palaestram contendērunt. turba ingēns in palaestrā erat. Quīntus   5
multōs iuvenēs, āthlētās, pugilēs cōnspexit. Quīntus multās
statuās in palaestrā vīdit.

"Pompēiānī āthlētīs nōtissimīs statuās posuērunt," inquit
Caecilius.

in palaestrā erat porticus ingēns. spectātōrēs in porticū stābant.   10
servī spectātōribus vīnum offerēbant.

Quīntus turbam prope porticum vīdit. āthlēta ingēns in mediā
turbā stābat.

"quis est āthlēta ille?" rogāvit Quīntus.

"ille est Milō, āthlēta nōtissimus," respondit Caecilius.   15

Caecilius et Quīntus ad Milōnem contendērunt.

Quīntus āthlētae discum novum ostendit. Milō, postquam
discum īnspexit, ad mediam palaestram prōcessit. āthlēta
palaestram circumspectāvit et discum ēmīsit. discus longē per
aurās ēvolāvit. spectātōrēs āthlētam laudāvērunt. servus Milōnī   20
discum quaesīvit. servus, postquam discum invēnit, ad Milōnem
rediit. servus āthlētae discum offerēbat. āthlēta tamen discum nōn
accēpit.

"discus nōn est meus," inquit Milō.

servus Quīntō discum trādidit. tum iuvenis quoque discum   25
ēmīsit. discus iterum per aurās ēvolāvit. discus tamen statuam
percussit.

"ēheu!" clāmāvit Caecilius. "statua nāsum frāctum habet."

Quīntus rīdēbat. Pompēiānī rīdēbant. Milō tamen nōn rīdēbat.

"cūr tū nōn rīdēs?" rogāvit iuvenis.   30

Milō erat īrātissimus.

"pestis!" respondit āthlēta. "mea est statua!"

statuās	statues	longē	far
posuērunt	have put up	per aurās ēvolāvit	flew through the air
porticus	colonnade	rediit	went back
offerēbant	were offering	nōn accēpit	did not accept
in mediā	in the middle of	trādidit	handed over
novum	new	nāsum frāctum	a broken nose

Questions

1 Why did Caecilius give Quintus a discus?
2 Where did Caecilius take Quintus? Suggest why they went there.
3 Who was in the crowd?
4 Why were there statues in the palaestra?
5 What were the slaves doing in the palaestra?
6 Write down two Latin words used in lines 12–15 to describe the athlete Milo. What do they tell us about him?
7 **āthlēta palaestram circumspectāvit**. Why do you think Milo did this before throwing the discus?
8 How did the spectators react in line 20? Why did they react in this way?
9 **discus nōn est meus** (line 24). What had just happened to make Milo say this?
10 In lines 26–28, what happened when Quintus threw the discus?
11 How was Milo's reaction different from that of the Pompeians (lines 29–32)? Do you think he was right to behave as he did? Why?

Palaestra of the Stabian Baths at Pompeii.

About the Language

A Study the following examples:

Clēmēns **puellae** vīnum offerēbat.
*Clemens was offering wine **to the girl**.*

iuvenis **servō** pecūniam trādidit.
*The young man handed over money **to the slave**.*

dominus **mercātōrī** statuam ēmit.
*The master bought a statue **for the merchant**.*

Grumiō **ancillīs** cēnam parāvit.
*Grumio prepared a dinner **for the slave-girls**.*

Quīntus **amīcīs** discum ostendit.
*Quintus showed the discus **to his friends**.*

servī **leōnibus** cibum dedērunt.
*The slaves gave food **to the lions**.*

The words in bold type are nouns in the **dative case**.

B You have now met three cases. Notice the different ways in which they are used:

nominative   **dominus** servō signum dedit.
            ***The master** gave a sign to the slave.*

dative   dominus **servō** signum dedit.
            *The master gave a sign **to the slave**.*

accusative   dominus servō **signum** dedit.
            *The master gave **a sign** to the slave.*

C Here is a full list of the noun endings that you have met. The new dative words are in bold type.

		FIRST DECLENSION	SECOND DECLENSION	THIRD DECLENSION
	nominative	puella	servus	mercātor
SINGULAR	*dative*	**puellae**	**servō**	**mercātōrī**
	accusative	puellam	servum	mercātōrem
	nominative	puellae	servī	mercātōrēs
PLURAL	*dative*	**puellīs**	**servīs**	**mercātōribus**
	accusative	puellās	servōs	mercātōrēs

D Further examples:

1 ancilla dominō cibum ostendit.
2 agricola uxōrī ānulum ēmit.
3 servus Metellae togam trādidit.
4 mercātor gladiātōribus pecūniam offerēbat.
5 fēmina ancillīs tunicās quaerēbat.

E Notice the different cases of the words for *I* and *you*:

ego senem salūtō.	*I greet the old man.*
frāter **mihi** statuam ostendit.	*My brother shows a statue to me.*
amīcus **mē** salūtat.	*The friend greets me.*
tū pictūram pingis.	*You are painting a picture.*
pater **tibi** pecūniam dat.	*Your father gives money to you.*
āthlēta **tē** laudat.	*The athlete praises you.*

nominative	ego	tū
dative	mihi	tibi
accusative	mē	tē

in tabernā

Metella et Melissa ē vīllā māne discessērunt. Metella fīliō togam
quaerēbat. Metella et ancilla, postquam forum intrāvērunt,
tabernam cōnspexērunt, ubi togae optimae erant. multae fēminae
erant in tabernā. servī fēminīs stolās ostendēbant. duo gladiātōrēs
quoque in tabernā erant. servī gladiātōribus tunicās ostendēbant.　　5
　　mercātor in mediā tabernā stābat. mercātor erat Marcellus.
Marcellus, postquam Metellam vīdit, rogāvit,
　　"quid quaeris, domina?"
　　"togam quaerō," inquit Metella. "ego fīliō dōnum quaerō, quod
diem nātālem celebrat."　　10
　　"ego multās togās habeō," respondit mercātor.
　　mercātor servīs signum dedit. servī mercātōrī togās celeriter
trādidērunt. Marcellus fēminīs togās ostendit. Metella et ancilla
togās īnspexērunt.

māne	*in the morning*	**dōnum**	*present, gift*
domina	*madam, ma'am*		

"hercle!" clāmāvit Melissa. "hae togae sunt sordidae." 15
Marcellus servōs vituperāvit.

"sunt intus togae splendidae," inquit Marcellus.

Marcellus fēminās intus dūxit. mercātor fēminīs aliās togās ostendit. Metella Quīntō mox togam splendidam ēlēgit.

"haec toga, quantī est?" rogāvit Metella. 20

"quīnquāgintā dēnāriōs cupiō," respondit Marcellus.

"quīnquāgintā dēnāriōs cupis! furcifer!" clāmāvit Melissa. "ego tibi decem dēnāriōs offerō."

"quadrāgintā dēnāriōs cupiō," respondit mercātor.

"tibi quīndecim dēnāriōs offerō," inquit ancilla. 25

"quid? haec est toga pulcherrima! quadrāgintā dēnāriōs cupiō," respondit Marcellus.

"tū nimium postulās," inquit Metella. "ego tibi trīgintā dēnāriōs dō."

"cōnsentiō," respondit Marcellus. 30

Melissa Marcellō pecūniam dedit. Marcellus Metellae togam trādidit.

"ego tibi grātiās maximās agō, domina," inquit Marcellus.

hae togae	*these togas*	**tibi**	*to you*
sordidae	*dirty*	**decem**	*ten*
intus	*inside*	**quadrāgintā**	*forty*
aliās	*other*	**quīndecim**	*fifteen*
ēlēgit	*chose*	**nimium**	*too much*
haec	*this*	**trīgintā**	*thirty*
quantī est?	*how much is it?*	**dō**	*give*
quīnquāgintā dēnāriōs	*fifty denarii*	**cōnsentiō**	*agree*
		ego ... grātiās ... agō	*thank, give thanks*
cupiō	*want*		

A fabric shop.

Practicing the Language

A Complete each sentence with a word that makes good sense, and then translate the sentence.

    For example: mercātōrēs fēminīs tunicās (audīvērunt, ostendērunt, timuērunt).
                      mercātōrēs fēminīs tunicās **ostendērunt**.
                      The merchants showed the tunics to the women.

1 ancilla dominō vīnum (timuit, dedit, salūtāvit).
2 iuvenis puellae stolam (ēmit, vēnit, prōcessit).
3 fēminae servīs tunicās (intrāvērunt, quaesīvērunt, contendērunt).
4 cīvēs āctōrī pecūniam (laudāvērunt, vocāvērunt, trādidērunt).
5 centuriō mercātōribus decem dēnāriōs (trādidit, ēmit, vīdit).

B Complete each sentence with the correct word, and then translate the sentence.

    For example: gladiātōrēs amīcīs tunicās (ostendit, ostendērunt).
                      gladiātōrēs amīcīs tunicās **ostendērunt**.
                      The gladiators showed the tunics to their friends.

1 puer gladiātōribus tunicās (dedit, dedērunt).
2 cīvēs Milōnī statuam (posuit, posuērunt).
3 mercātor amīcō vīnum (trādidit, trādidērunt).
4 coquus ancillae ānulum (ēmit, ēmērunt).
5 vēnālīciī fēminīs servōs (ostendit, ostendērunt).
6 servus Quīntō discum (quaesīvit, quaesīvērunt).
7 nautae uxōribus stolās pulchrās (ēlēgit, ēlēgērunt).
8 Clēmēns et Grumiō Metellae cēnam optimam (parāvit, parāvērunt).

C The following words all occur (in this order) in the story, **in tabernā** (pages 149–50.) They are either accusative plural or dative plural. Divide them into two lists according to their case.

fēminīs stolās gladiātōribus tunicās togās servīs servōs fēminās dēnāriōs grātiās

in apodytēriō

duo servī in apodytēriō stant. servī sunt Sceledrus et Anthrāx.

Sceledrus: cūr nōn labōrās, Anthrāx? num dormīs?

Anthrāx: quid dīcis? dīligenter labōrō. ego cīvibus togās custōdiō.

Sceledrus: togās custōdīs? mendāx es!

Anthrāx: cūr mē vituperās? mendāx nōn sum. togās custōdiō.

Sceledrus: tē vituperō, quod fūr est in apodytēriō, sed tū nihil facis.

Anthrāx: ubi est fūr? fūrem nōn videō.

Sceledrus: ecce! homō ille est fūr. fūrem facile agnōscō. (*Sceledrus Anthrācī fūrem ostendit. fūr togam suam dēpōnit et togam splendidam induit. servī ad fūrem statim currunt.*)

Anthrāx: quid facis? furcifer! haec toga nōn est tua!

fūr: mendāx es! mea est toga! abī!

Sceledrus: tē agnōscō! pauper es, sed togam splendidam geris. (*mercātor intrat. togam frūstrā quaerit.*)

mercātor: ēheu! ubi est toga mea? toga ēvānuit! (*mercātor circumspectat.*) ecce! hic fūr togam meam gerit!

fūr: parce! parce! pauperrimus sum … uxor mea est aegra … decem līberōs habeō …

mercātor et servī fūrem nōn audiunt, sed eum ad iūdicem trahunt.

induit *is putting on*
abī! *go away!*
pauper *a poor man*
geris *you are wearing*
parce! *spare me!*
aegra *sick, ill*
līberōs *children*
audiunt *listen to*

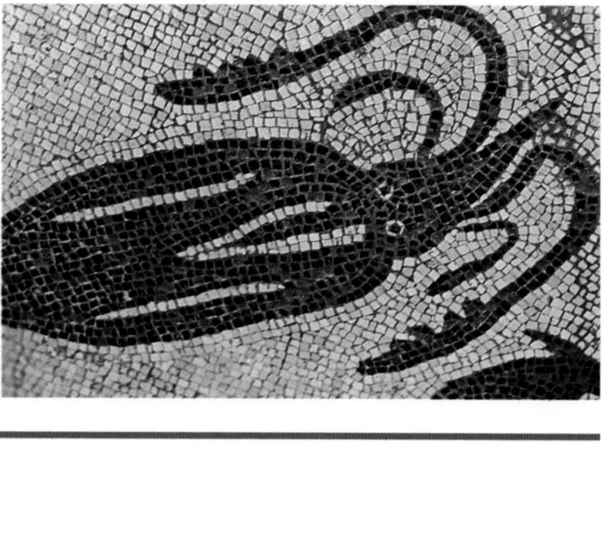

This mosaic of a squid is in an apodyterium in Herculaneum.

An apodyterium in the women's section of the Stabian Baths at Pompeii.

The caldarium in the Forum Baths, Pompeii. At the nearer end note the large rectangular marble bath, which was filled with hot water. At the far end there is a labrum, a stone basin for cold water. Rooms in baths often had grooved, curved ceilings to channel condensation down the walls.

The Baths

About the middle of the afternoon, Caecilius would make his way, with a group of friends, to the public baths. The great majority of Pompeians did not have rooms with baths in their houses, so they went regularly to the public baths to keep themselves clean. As at a leisure center, city pool, or health club today, they could also exercise, meet friends, and have a snack. Let us imagine that Caecilius decides to visit the baths situated just to the north of the forum, and let us follow him through the various rooms and activities.

At one of the entrances, he pays a small admission fee to the **ōstiārius** (doorkeeper) and then goes to the **palaestra** (exercise area). This is an open space surrounded by a colonnade, rather like a large peristylium. Here he spends a little time greeting other friends and taking part in some of the popular exercises, which included throwing a large ball from one to another, wrestling, and fencing with wooden swords. These games were not taken too seriously but were a pleasant preparation for the bath which followed.

From the palaestra, Caecilius and his friends walk along a passage into a large hall known as the **apodytērium** (changing room). Here they undress and hand their clothes to one of the slave attendants who places them in recesses arranged in rows along the wall.

Leaving the apodyterium, they pass through an arched doorway into the **tepidārium** (warm room) and spend a little time sitting on benches around the wall in a warm, steamy atmosphere, perspiring gently and preparing for the higher temperatures in the next room.

This is the **caldārium** (hot room). At one end of the caldarium, there was a large marble bath, rectangular in shape and stretching across the full width of the room. This bath was filled with hot water in which the bathers sat or wallowed. The Romans did not have soap but used olive oil instead. After soaking in the bath, Caecilius summons a slave to rub him down with the oil that he has brought with him in a little pot. For this rubbing down, Caecilius lies on a marble slab while the slave works the oil into his skin and then gently removes it and the dirt with a blunt metal scraper known as a **strigil**. Next comes the masseur to massage skin and muscles. Refreshed by this treatment, Caecilius then goes to the large stone basin at the other end of the caldarium for a refreshing splash or rinse with cold water.

Before dressing again, he might well visit the **frigidārium** (cold room) and there take a plunge in a deep circular pool of unheated water, followed by a brisk rub down with his towel.

Caecilius' visit to the baths was a leisurely social occasion. He enjoyed a noisy, relaxed time in the company of his friends. The Roman writer Seneca lived uncomfortably close to a set of baths in Rome, and his description gives us a vivid impression of the atmosphere there:

> I am surrounded by uproar. I live over a set of baths. Just imagine the babel of sounds that strikes my ears. When the athletic gentlemen below are exercising themselves, lifting lead weights, I can hear their grunts. I can hear the whistling of their breath as it escapes from their lungs. I can hear somebody enjoying a cheap rub down and the smack of the masseur's hands on his shoulders. If his hand comes down flat, it makes one sound; if it comes down hollowed, it makes another. Add to this the noise of a brawler or thief being arrested down below, the racket made by the man who likes to sing in his bath or the sound of enthusiasts who hurl themselves into the water with a tremendous splash. Next I can hear the screech of the hair-plucker, who advertises himself by shouting. He is never quiet except when he is plucking hair and making his victim shout instead. Finally, just imagine the cries of the cake-seller, the sausage-man, and the other food-sellers as they advertise their goods around the bath, all adding to the din.

A bronze statue of a boxer from a set of baths in Rome. His training would no doubt have contributed to the din about which Seneca complains.

A Visit to the Baths

These pictures show us a bather's route through the different rooms of the bath complex after he leaves the palaestra.

They are taken from several different sets of baths, as no one set has all its rooms well preserved today.

1 *The entrance hall with the apodyterium beyond.*
Stabian Baths, Pompeii.

2 *The tepidarium. This sometimes had recesses for clothes like the apodyterium.*
Forum Baths, Pompeii.

3 *The hot tub in the caldarium.*
Herculaneum.

4 *The caldarium, showing a marble bench for sitting or massage.*
Herculaneum.

5 *The frigidarium: cold plunge bath.*
Forum Baths, Pompeii.

Heating the Baths

The Romans were not the first people to build public baths. This was one of the many things they learned from the Greeks. But with their engineering skill the Romans greatly improved the methods of heating them. The previous method had been to heat the water in tanks over a furnace, and to stand braziers (portable metal containers in which wood was burned) in the tepidarium and the caldarium to keep up the air temperature. The braziers were not very efficient, and they failed to heat the floor.

In the first century B.C., a Roman invented the first central heating system. The furnace was placed below the floor level; the floor was supported on small brick piles leaving space through which hot air from the furnace could circulate. In this way, the floor was warmed from below. The caldarium was located near the furnace and a steady temperature was maintained by the hot air passing immediately below. By the time of our stories, flues (channels) were built into the walls, and warm air from beneath the floor was drawn up through them. This ingenious heating system was known as a **hypocaust**. It was used not only in baths but also in private houses, particularly in the colder parts of the Roman Empire such as Britain. Wood was the fuel most commonly burned in the furnaces.

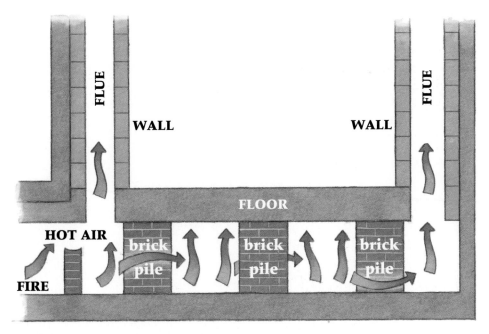

A hypocaust viewed from the side.

Plan of the Forum Baths, Pompeii

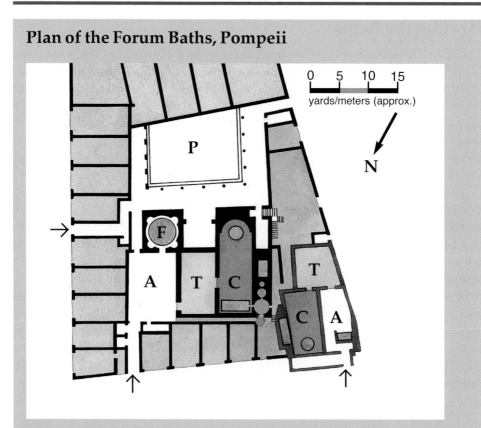

The men's section is outlined in black and the women's in blue. See how the hottest rooms (red) in both suites are arranged on either side of the one furnace (marked by an orange dot). The blue circles near this are boilers. After losing some heat to the hot rooms the hot air goes on to warm the warm rooms (pink).

Key

P: palaestra
A: apodyterium
T: tepidarium
C: caldarium
F: frigidarium

The small arrows mark public entrances. The orange spaces are shops.

Word Study

A Match each definition with one of the words given below:

civilization   homicide   ostensible
emission   hospital   reiterate
exercise

1 . . . . .   seeming; apparent
2 . . . . .   a giving off or sending out
3 . . . . .   to repeat
4 . . . . .   human society
5 . . . . .   murder
6 . . . . .   to engage in vigorous physical activity
7 . . . . .   a building used to house and treat sick persons

B Using the word bank supplied, give the derivative that is implied in the following phrases:

accelerator   conference   ostentatious
traditions   dismal

1 Having a **bad day**, you might feel . . . . .
2 Customs **handed down** from one generation to the next are the primary source of . . . . .
3 **Bring together** both sides to discuss their issues; hold a . . . . .
4 A person who is **showy** and pretentious is . . . . .
5 To drive **more quickly**, depress the . . . . .

Hypocaust in the Stabian Baths. Notice the floor supported by brick pillars so that hot air can circulate beneath and warm both the room and the tank of water for bathing.

Stage 9
Vocabulary Checklist

agnōscit: agnōvit	*recognizes*
celebrat: celebrāvit	*celebrates*
celeriter	*quickly*
cīvis: cīvem	*citizen*
cupit: cupīvit	*wants*
dat: dedit	*gives*
diēs	*day*
diēs nātālis	*birthday*
ēmittit: ēmīsit	*throws, sends out*
exercet: exercuit	*exercises*
fert: tulit	*brings, carries*
homō: hominem	*person, man*
hospes: hospitem	*guest*
ille	*that*
īnspicit: īnspexit	*looks at, inspects, examines*
iterum	*again*
manet: mānsit	*remains, stays*
medius	*middle*
mox	*soon*
nōtus	*well-known, famous*
offert: obtulit	*offers*
ostendit: ostendit	*shows*
paulīsper	*for a short time*
post	*after*
revenit: revēnit	*comes back, returns*
suus	*his*
trādit: trādidit	*hands over*

The floors of baths often had marine themes. This mosaic of an octopus is in the women's baths at Herculaneum.

RHETOR

Stage 10

1 Rōmānus dīcit,
  "nōs Rōmānī sumus architectī. nōs viās et pontēs aedificāmus."

2 "nōs Rōmānī sumus agricolae. nōs fundōs optimōs habēmus."

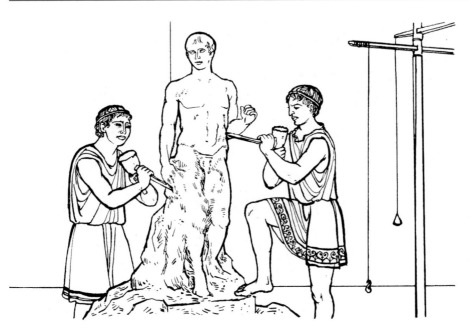

3 Graecus dīcit,
   "nōs Graecī sumus sculptōrēs. nōs statuās pulchrās facimus."

4 "nōs Graecī sumus pictōrēs. nōs pictūrās pingimus."

5 Rōmānus dīcit,
  "vōs Graecī estis ignāvī. vōs āctōrēs semper spectātis."

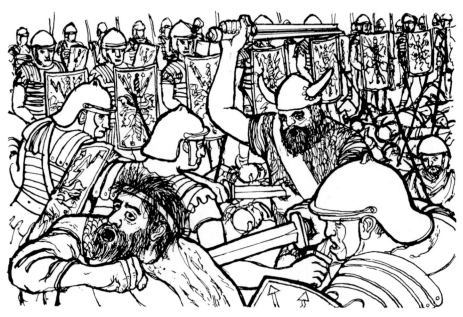

6 Graecus dīcit,
  "vōs Rōmānī estis barbarī. vōs semper pugnātis."

7 Rōmānus dīcit,
  "nōs sumus callidī. nōs rēs ūtilēs facimus."

8 Graecus dīcit,
  "nōs sumus callidiōrēs quam vōs. nōs Graecī Rōmānōs docēmus."

contrōversia

Quīntus amīcum Graecum habēbat. amīcus erat Alexander.
Quīntus et Alexander ad palaestram ībant, ubi rhētor Graecus erat.
hic rhētor erat Theodōrus et prope palaestram habitābat. in
palaestrā erat porticus longa, ubi Theodōrus iuvenēs docēbat.
postquam ad hanc porticum vēnērunt, Alexander et Quīntus   5
rhētorem audīvērunt. rhētor iuvenibus contrōversiam nūntiāvit:
"Graecī sunt meliōrēs quam Rōmānī."

   Quīntus vehementer exclāmāvit,
   "minimē! nōs Rōmānī sumus meliōrēs quam Graecī."
   Theodōrus, postquam hanc sententiam audīvit, respondit,   10
   "haec est tua sententia. nōs tamen nōn sententiam quaerimus,
nōs argūmentum quaerimus."

   tum Quīntus rhētorī et amīcīs argūmentum explicāvit.
   "nōs Rōmānī sumus fortissimī. nōs barbarōs ferōcissimōs
superāmus. nōs imperium maximum habēmus. nōs pācem   15
servāmus. vōs Graecī semper contentiōnēs habētis. vōs semper
estis turbulentī.

   "nōs sumus architectī optimī. nōs viās et pontēs ubīque
aedificāmus. urbs Rōma est māior quam omnēs aliae urbēs.

   "postrēmō nōs Rōmānī dīligenter labōrāmus. deī igitur nōbīs   20
imperium maximum dant. vōs Graecī estis ignāvī. vōs numquam
labōrātis. deī vōbīs nihil dant."

   postquam Quīntus hanc sententiam explicāvit, iuvenēs
Pompēiānī vehementer plausērunt et eum laudāvērunt. deinde
Alexander surrēxit. iuvenēs Pompēiānī tacuērunt et Alexandrum   25
intentē spectāvērunt.

   "vōs Rōmānī estis miserandī. vōs
imperium maximum habētis, sed vōs
estis imitātōrēs; nōs Graecī sumus
auctōrēs. vōs Graecās statuās spectātis,   30
vōs Graecōs librōs legitis, Graecōs
rhētorēs audītis. vōs Rōmānī estis
rīdiculī, quod estis Graeciōrēs quam
nōs Graecī!"

   iuvenēs, postquam Alexander   35
sententiam suam explicāvit, rīsērunt.
tum Theodōrus nūntiāvit,
   "Alexander victor est. argūmentum
optimum explicāvit."

contrōversia	debate	aedificāmus	build
rhētor	teacher	maior quam	greater than, bigger than
docēbat	used to teach		
hanc	this	aliae	other
meliōrēs quam	better than	postrēmō	lastly
minimē!	no!	deī	gods
sententiam	opinion	dant	give
argūmentum	proof	deinde	then
barbarōs	barbarians	surrēxit	got up
imperium	empire	miserandī	pathetic, pitiful
pācem	peace	imitātōrēs	imitators
architectī	builders, architects	auctōrēs	creators
		librōs	books
pontēs	bridges	legitis	read
ubīque	everywhere	rīsērunt	laughed

The Romans built this bridge at Alcantara in Spain.

statuae

postquam Theodōrus Alexandrum laudāvit, iuvenēs Pompēiānī ē
porticū discessērunt. Alexander et Quīntus ad vīllam ambulābant,
ubi Alexander et duo frātrēs habitābant.

Alexander frātribus dōnum quaerēbat, quod diem nātālem
celebrābant.   5

in viā īnstitor parvās statuās vēndēbat et clāmābat:
"statuae! optimae statuae!"
Alexander frātribus statuās ēmit. statuae erant senex, iuvenis,
puella pulchra. Alexander, postquam statuās ēmit, ad vīllam cum
Quīntō contendit.   10

duo frātrēs in hortō sedēbant. Diodōrus pictūram pingēbat,
Thrasymachus librum Graecum legēbat. postquam Alexander et
Quīntus vīllam intrāvērunt, puerī ad eōs cucurrērunt. Diodōrus
statuās cōnspexit.

"Alexander, quid portās?" inquit.   15
"vōs estis fēlīcēs," inquit Alexander. "ego vōbīs dōnum habeō
quod vōs diem nātālem celebrātis. ecce!" Alexander frātribus
statuās ostendit.

"quam pulchra est puella!" inquit Diodōrus. "dā mihi
puellam!"   20
"minimē! frāter, dā mihi puellam!" clāmāvit Thrasymachus.
puerī dissentiēbant et lacrimābant.
"hercle! vōs estis stultissimī puerī!" clāmāvit Alexander īrātus.
"semper dissentītis, semper lacrimātis. abīte! abīte! ego statuās
retineō!"   25

puerī, postquam Alexander hoc dīxit, abiērunt. Diodōrus
pictūram in terram dēiēcit, quod īrātus erat. Thrasymachus librum
in piscīnam dēiēcit, quod īrātissimus erat.

tum Quīntus dīxit,
"Alexander, dā mihi statuās! Thrasymache! Diodōre! venīte   30
hūc! Thrasymache, ecce! ego tibi senem dō, quod senex erat
philosophus. Diodōre, tibi iuvenem dō, quod iuvenis erat pictor.
ego mihi puellam dō, quod ego sum sōlus! vōsne estis contentī?"
"sumus contentī," respondērunt puerī.
"ecce, Alexander," inquit Quīntus, "vōs Graeculī estis optimī   35
artificēs sed turbulentī. nōs Rōmānī vōbīs pācem damus."
"et vōs praemium accipitis," susurrāvit Thrasymachus.

frātrēs	brothers
īnstitor	pedlar, street vendor
ad eōs	to them
fēlīcēs	lucky
quam!	how!
dā!	give!
dissentiēbant	were arguing
stultissimī	very stupid
abīte!	go away!
retineō	am keeping
abiērunt	went away
in terram	onto the ground
dēiēcit	threw
in piscīnam	into the fishpond
venīte hūc!	come here!
philosophus	philosopher
sōlus	lonely
vōsne estis contentī?	are you satisfied?
Graeculī	poor little Greeks
artificēs	artists
praemium	profit, reward
susurrāvit	whispered, muttered

Greek writers and thinkers have influenced people's minds to this day;
above left: the tragic dramatist Euripides; above right: the philosopher
Anaximander, who taught that the universe was governed by law.
He is holding a sundial, which he is said to have invented.

About the Language I

A In this Stage, you have met sentences with *we* and *you*:

>nōs labōrāmus. *We work.*
>vōs labōrātis. *You work.*

Notice that **vōs labōrātis** is the plural form. It is used when *you* refers to more than one person.

B You have now met the whole of the present tense:

(ego)	portō	*I carry, I am carrying*
(tū)	portās	*you (singular) carry, you are carrying*
	portat	*s/he carries, s/he is carrying*
(nōs)	portāmus	*we carry, we are carrying*
(vōs)	portātis	*you (plural) carry, you are carrying*
	portant	*they carry, they are carrying*

C Notice that **nōs** and **vōs** are not strictly necessary, since the endings **-mus** and **-tis** make it clear that *we* and *you* are being spoken about. The Romans generally used **nōs** and **vōs** only for emphasis.

D Further examples:

1 nōs pugnāmus. vōs dormītis.
2 dīcimus. vidēmus. vidētis. nūntiātis.

E The Latin for *we are* and *you (plural) are* is as follows:

>**nōs sumus** iuvenēs. *We are young men.*
>**vōs estis** pictōrēs. *You are painters.*

So the complete present tense of **sum** is:

(ego)	sum	*I am*
(tū)	es	*you (singular) are*
	est	*s/he is*
(nōs)	sumus	*we are*
(vōs)	estis	*you (plural) are*
	sunt	*they are*

About the Language II

A Study the following pairs of sentences:

> nōs Rōmānī sumus callidī.
> *We Romans are clever.*

> nōs Rōmānī sumus **callidiōrēs** quam vōs Graecī.
> *We Romans are **cleverer** than you Greeks.*

> nōs Rōmānī sumus fortēs.
> *We Romans are brave.*

> nōs Rōmānī sumus **fortiōrēs** quam vōs Graecī.
> *We Romans are **braver** than you Greeks.*

The words in bold type are known as **comparatives**. They are used to compare two things or groups with each other. In the examples above, the Romans are comparing themselves with the Greeks.

B Further examples:

1 Pompēiānī sunt stultī. Nūcerīnī sunt stultiōrēs quam Pompēiānī.
2 Diodōrus erat īrātus, sed Thrasymachus erat īrātior quam Diodōrus.
3 mea vīlla est pulchra, sed tua vīlla est pulchrior quam mea.

C The following words form their comparatives in an unusual way:

> Nūceria est **magna**.   Rōma est **maior** quam Nūceria.
> *Nuceria is large.*   *Rome is larger than Nuceria.*

> sententia tua est **bona**.   sententia mea est **melior** quam tua.
> *Your opinion is good.*   *My opinion is better than yours.*

ānulus Aegyptius

When you have read this story, answer the questions opposite.

Syphāx in tabernā sedēbat. caupō Syphācī vīnum dedit. Syphāx caupōnī ānulum trādidit.

"pecūniam nōn habeō," inquit, "quod Neptūnus nāvem meam dēlēvit."

caupō, postquam ānulum accēpit, eum īnspexit.   5

"ānulus antīquus est," inquit.

"ita vērō, antīquus est," Syphāx caupōnī respondit. "servus Aegyptius mihi ānulum dedit. servus in pȳramide ānulum invēnit."

caupō, postquam tabernam clausit, ad vīllam suam festīnāvit. 10
caupō uxōrī ānulum ostendit. caupō uxōrī ānulum dedit, quod ānulus eam dēlectāvit.

uxor postrīdiē ad urbem contendēbat. subitō servus ingēns in viā appāruit. pecūniam postulāvit. fēmina, quod erat perterrita, servō pecūniam dedit. servus ānulum cōnspexit. ānulum 15
postulāvit. fēmina servō eum trādidit.

fēmina ad tabernam rediit et marītum quaesīvit. mox eum invēnit. caupō incendium spectābat. ēheu! taberna ardēbat! fēmina marītō rem tōtam nārrāvit.

"ānulus īnfēlīx est," inquit caupō. "ānulus tabernam meam 20
dēlēvit."

servus ingēns, postquam pecūniam et ānulum cēpit, ad urbem contendit. subitō trēs servōs cōnspexit. servī inimīcī erant. inimīcī, postquam pecūniam cōnspexērunt, servum verberābant. servus fūgit, sed ānulum āmīsit. 25

Grumiō cum Poppaeā ambulābat. ānulum in viā invēnit.

"quid vidēs?" rogāvit Poppaea.

"ānulum videō," inquit. "ānulus Aegyptius est."

"euge!" inquit Poppaea. "ānulus fēlīx est."

Aegyptius	*Egyptian*	**clausit**	*shut, closed*
caupō	*innkeeper*	**eam**	*her*
Neptūnus	*Neptune*	**marītum**	*husband*
	(god of the sea)	**incendium**	*blaze, fire*
dēlēvit	*has destroyed*	**ardēbat**	*was on fire*
antīquus	*old, ancient*	**īnfēlīx**	*unlucky*
in pȳramide	*in a pyramid*	**āmīsit**	*lost*

Questions

1. How did Syphax pay for his drink?
2. Why did he pay in this way?
3. What do you think he meant in lines 3–4 by saying **Neptūnus nāvem meam dēlēvit**?
4. In lines 7–9, Syphax gave three other pieces of information about the ring. What were they?
5. What two things did the innkeeper do with the ring?
6. What did the innkeeper's wife do the next day? Whom did she meet? What two things did he make her do?
7. What did she find when she returned to the inn (line 18)?
8. What three things happened after the huge slave met the other slaves and they spotted the money (lines 23–25)?
9. Who found the ring?
10. Write a paragraph describing what you think will happen next to Grumio and Poppaea.

*Bronze ring decorated with the heads of
Egyptian gods Isis and Serapis.*

Practicing the Language

A Complete each sentence with the most suitable phrase from the list below, and then translate it.

> fābulam agimus   stolās compōnimus
> contrōversiam habēmus   pānem parāmus
> cibum offerimus

  1 nōs sumus rhētōrēs Graecī; nōs in palaestrā . . . . . .
  2 nōs sumus āctōrēs nōtissimī; nōs in theātrō . . . . . .
  3 nōs sumus ancillae pulchrae; nōs fēminīs . . . . . .
  4 nōs sumus coquī; nōs dominīs . . . . . .
  5 nōs sumus pistōrēs; nōs cīvibus . . . . . .

B Complete each sentence with the most suitable word from the list below, and then translate it.

> servī   vēnāliciī
> āthlētae   gladiātōrēs
> pictōrēs

  1 vōs estis . . . . . callidī; vōs pictūrās magnificās pingitis.
  2 vōs estis . . . . . fortēs; vōs in arēnā pugnātis.
  3 nōs sumus . . . . . ; nōs in thermīs togās custōdīmus.
  4 vōs servōs in forō vēnditis, quod vōs estis . . . . . .
  5 nōs ad palaestram contendimus, quod nōs sumus . . . . . .

C Refer to the story **statuae** on page 168, and complete each sentence according to that story. Then translate each sentence.

  1 Alexander (frātribus, frātrī) trēs statuās ēmit.
  2 Alexander (puerō, puerīs) statuās ostendit.
  3 "dā (mihi, tibi) puellam," clāmāvit Diodōrus.
  4 Quīntus, postquam frātrēs dissentiēbant et lacrimābant, (Diodōrō, Thrasymachō) senem trādidit.
  5 Quīntus (pictōribus, pictōrī) iuvenem offert.
  6 "Rōmānī," inquit Quīntus, "(Graeculō turbulentō, Graeculīs turbulentīs) pācem dant."

Education

Boys and girls grew up together, sharing their activities and games. Until the age of seven, they had lessons from their mothers who taught them to speak Latin correctly and to do elementary reading and writing. At seven the boys were sent to school. Sometimes girls went too, but generally they would stay at home. In upper-class families, some girls continued their education privately with a tutor with whom they studied Greek and Latin literature and learned to play the lyre and sing. Most of their time would be spent learning the skills of a good housewife: cooking, cleaning, childcare, and, perhaps, spinning and weaving. Girls from wealthy families would learn to organize a household of slaves.

The First Stage of Education

Quintus would have first gone to school when he was about seven years old. Like other Roman schools, the one that Quintus attended would have been small and consisted of about thirty pupils and a teacher known as the **lūdī magister**. All the teaching would take place in a rented room or perhaps in a public colonnade or square, where there would be constant noise and distractions.

Parents were not obliged by law to send their children to school, and those who wanted education for their children had to pay for it. The charges were not high, and the advantages of being able to read and write were so widely appreciated that many people were prepared to pay for their sons to go to school at least for a few years.

On the journey between home and school, pupils were normally escorted by a slave known as a **paedagōgus** who was responsible for their behavior and protection. Another slave carried their books and writing materials.

Two boys and their teacher at school. The boys are using papyrus rolls.

At the school of the *ludi magister* Quintus would have learned to read and write Latin and Greek and perhaps to do some simple arithmetic. Like most Roman boys he would already be able to speak some Greek, which he would have picked up from Greek slaves at home or from friends like Alexander in the story.

Writing Materials

The materials that Quintus used for writing were rather different from ours. Frequently he wrote on **tabulae** (wooden tablets) coated with a thin film of wax and he inscribed the letters on the wax surface with a thin stick of metal, bone, or ivory. This stick was called a **stilus**. The end opposite the writing point was flat so that it could be used to rub out mistakes and make the wax smooth again. Several tablets were strung together to make a little writing-book. At other times he wrote with ink on papyrus, a material that looked rather like modern paper but was rougher in texture. It was manufactured from the fibers of the papyrus reed that grew along the banks of the River Nile in Egypt. For writing on papyrus he used either a reed or a goose-quill sharpened and split at one end like the modern pen-nib. Ink was made from soot and resin or other gummy substances, forming a paste that was thinned by adding water. The best inks were so hard and durable that they are perfectly legible even today on the pieces of papyrus that have survived.

Pictures of scenes in school show that there were generally no desks and no blackboard. Pupils sat on benches or stools, resting tablets on their knees. The master sat on a high chair overlooking his class. Discipline was usually strict and sometimes harsh.

The school day began early and lasted for six hours with a short break at midday. Holidays were given on public festivals and on every ninth

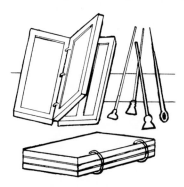

tabulae et stili.

Papyrus rolls, a double inkwell (for red and black ink) and a quill pen. From a Pompeian painting.

day which was a market-day; during the hot summer months, fewer pupils attended lessons, and some schoolmasters may have closed their schools altogether from July to October.

A wax tablet with a student's exercise in Greek. The master has written the top two lines, and the child has copied them below.

The Second Stage

Many children would have finished their schooling at the age of eleven, but a boy like Quintus from a wealthy family would have moved to a more advanced school run by a **grammaticus**. The *grammaticus* introduced his pupils to the works of famous Greek and Roman writers, beginning with the *Iliad* and *Odyssey* of Homer. Then the pupils moved on to the tragedies of Aeschylus, Sophocles, and Euripides, famous Greek playwrights whose plays had first been performed in Athens in the fifth century B.C. The Roman poets most frequently read at school were Vergil and Horace. Besides reading works of literature aloud, the pupils had to analyze the grammar and learn long passages by heart; many educated people could remember these passages in later life and quote or recite them. The pupils were also taught a little history and geography, mainly in order to understand references to famous people and places mentioned in the literature.

The poet Vergil.

When he left the *grammaticus* at the age of fifteen or sixteen, Quintus would have had a very good knowledge of Greek as well as Latin. This knowledge of Greek not only introduced the students to a culture which the Romans greatly admired and which had inspired much of their own civilization, but was also very useful in later life because Greek was widely spoken in the countries of the eastern Mediterranean where Roman merchants and government officials frequently traveled on business.

The Third Stage

A few students then proceeded to the school of a **rhētor**, like Theodorus in our story. This teacher, who was often a highly educated Greek, gave more advanced lessons in literature and trained his students in the art of public speaking. This was a very important skill for young men who expected to take part in public life. They needed it to present cases in the law courts, to express their opinions in town council meetings, and to address the people at election time. The rhetor taught the rules for making different kinds of speeches and made his students practice arguing for and against a point of view. Students also learned how to vary their tone of voice and emphasize their words with gestures.

Science and Technical Subjects

We have not so far mentioned the teaching of science and technical subjects in Roman schools. It is true that the Greeks had made important discoveries in mathematics and some aspects of physics. It is also true that the Romans were experienced in such things as the methods of surveying and the use of concrete in building. But these things played little part in school work. The purpose of ordinary Roman schools was to teach those things which were thought to be most necessary for civilized living: the ability to read and write, a knowledge of simple arithmetic, the appreciation of fine literature, and the ability to speak and argue convincingly. Science and advanced mathematics were taught to only a few students whose parents were interested and wealthy enough to pay the fees of a specialist teacher, nearly always a Greek. Technical skills were learned by becoming an apprentice in a trade or business.

Apprentices carving a table leg.

Word Study

A Give the Latin word from which these words are derived:

1 susceptible
2 pronouncement
3 sentence
4 reservoir
5 fraternize
6 transit
7 inimical
8 pacify
9 invention
10 tacit

B Match the derivative and its meaning:

1 vehement   **a** a speech given alone, a monologue
2 capacious   **b** roomy, able to contain a large quantity
3 enmity   **c** taking a long or indirect course
4 inventive   **d** forceful, energetic
5 circuitous   **e** deep-seated hatred as between enemies
6 reticent   **f** skilled in finding new methods, creative
7 soliloquy   **g** a collection of books
8 library   **h** characteristically silent

C Copy the following words. Then put parentheses around the Latin root from this Stage contained inside these derivatives; give the Latin word and its meaning from which the derivative comes.

For example: con(serv)atory – servat – saves

1 incapacitate
2 importune
3 taciturn
4 pacific
5 libel
6 pronunciation
7 preservative
8 desolation
9 uxorious
10 fraternity

Stage 10
Vocabulary Checklist

abit: abiit	*goes away*
accipit: accēpit	*accepts, receives*
callidus	*clever, smart*
capit: cēpit	*takes*
contentus	*satisfied*
exclāmat: exclāmāvit	*exclaims*
frāter: frātrem	*brother*
imperium	*empire*
inimīcus	*enemy*
invenit: invēnit	*finds*
it: iit	*goes*
liber: librum	*book*
nōs	*we*
nūntiat: nūntiāvit	*announces*
pāx: pācem	*peace*
portus	*harbor*
quam	*than, how*
semper	*always*
sententia	*opinion*
servat: servāvit	*saves, protects*
sōlus	*alone, lonely*
tacet: tacuit	*is silent, is quiet*
uxor: uxōrem	*wife*
vehementer	*violently, loudly*
vōs	*you (plural)*

A pen (made from a reed), inkwell, papyrus roll, stilus and wax tablets.

CANDIDATI

Stage 11

1 cīvēs in forō candidātōs spectant.

2 agricolae clāmant,
"nōs candidātum optimum
habēmus."
"candidātus noster est Lūcius."
"nōs Lūciō favēmus."

3 mercātōrēs agricolīs respondent,
"nōs candidātum optimum
habēmus."
"candidātus noster est mercātor."
"nōs mercātōrī favēmus."

4 pistōrēs in forō clāmant,
  "nōs pistōrēs candidātum
    optimum habēmus."
  "candidātus noster est pistor."
  "nōs pistōrī crēdimus."

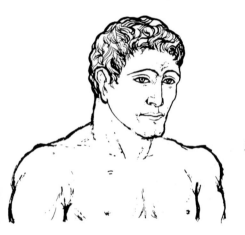

5 iuvenēs pistōribus respondent,
  "nōs iuvenēs candidātum
    optimum habēmus."
  "candidātus noster est āthlēta."
  "nōs āthlētae crēdimus."

6 fūrēs clāmant,
  "nōs quoque candidātum
    habēmus."
  "candidātus noster est fūr."
  "nōs candidātō nostrō nōn
    crēdimus sed favēmus."

Marcus et Quārtus

Marcus Tullius et Quārtus Tullius erant frātrēs. Marcus et Quārtus in vīllā contentiōnem habēbant. Marcus Quārtō dīxit,

"Āfer candidātus optimus est. Āfer multās vīllās et multās tabernās habet. Pompēiānī Āfrō favent, quod vir dīves est."

"minimē! Holcōnius candidātus optimus est," Quārtus frātrī respondit. "Holcōnius est vir nōbilis. Pompēiānī Holcōniō crēdunt, quod pater senātor erat." 5

Quārtus, quod erat īrātissimus, ē vīllā discessit. Quārtus sibi dīxit,

"frāter meus est stultissimus. gēns nostra Holcōniō semper favet." 10

Quārtus per viam ambulābat et rem cōgitābat. subitō parvam tabernam cōnspexit, ubi scrīptor habitābat. scrīptor Sulla erat. Quārtus, postquam tabernam vīdit, cōnsilium cēpit. tabernam intrāvit et Sullam ad vīllam suam invītāvit. 15

postquam ad vīllam vēnērunt, Quārtus Sullae mūrum ostendit.

"scrībe hunc titulum!" inquit. "scrībe 'Quārtus et frāter Holcōniō favent. Quārtus et frāter Holcōniō crēdunt.' "

Quārtus scrīptōrī decem dēnāriōs dedit.

"placetne tibi?" rogāvit Quārtus. 20

"mihi placet," Sulla Quārtō respondit. Sulla, postquam dēnāriōs accēpit, titulum in mūrō scrīpsit.

candidātus	*candidate*
favent	*favor, give support to*
vir dīves	*a rich man*
vir nōbilis	*a man of noble birth*
crēdunt	*trust, have faith in*
sibi dīxit	*said to himself*
gēns nostra	*our family*
rem cōgitābat	*was considering the problem*
scrīptor	*sign-writer*
cōnsilium cēpit	*had an idea*
mūrum	*wall*
scrībe!	*write!*
titulum	*notice, slogan*
placetne tibi?	*does it suit you? is it okay with you?*
scrīpsit	*wrote*

Sulla

Marcus ē vīllā vēnit. Sullam vīdit. titulum cōnspexit. postquam titulum lēgit, īrātus erat. Marcus scrīptōrem valdē vituperāvit.

"frāter tuus mē ad vīllam invītāvit," inquit Sulla. "frāter tuus mihi decem dēnāriōs dedit."

"frāter meus est stultior quam asinus," Marcus Sullae   5
respondit. "in vīllā nostrā ego sum dominus, quod sum senior. Sulla, ērāde illam īnscrīptiōnem! scrībe titulum novum!"

Marcus Sullae quīndecim dēnāriōs dedit.

"placetne tibi?" rogāvit.

"mihi placet," Sulla Marcō respondit. Sulla, postquam   10
īnscrīptiōnem ērāsit, hunc titulum scrīpsit, "Marcus et frāter Āfrō favent. Marcus et frāter Āfrō crēdunt."

Marcus erat laetissimus et frātrem ē vīllā vocāvit. Marcus frātrī titulum novum ostendit. Quārtus, postquam titulum lēgit, īrātus erat. Quārtus Marcum pulsāvit. tum frātrēs in viā pugnābant!   15

"Marce! Quārte! dēsistite! intrō īte!" clāmāvit Sulla. "cōnsilium optimum habeō."

postquam frātrēs vīllam intrāvērunt, Sulla celeriter rem cōnfēcit.

duōs titulōs in mūrō scrīpsit. tum frātrēs ē vīllā vocāvit.   20

scrīptor frātribus mūrum ostendit. ecce! Marcus hunc titulum vīdit: "Marcus Āfrō favet. Āfer est candidātus optimus."

"euge! hic titulus mē valdē dēlectat," inquit Marcus.

Quārtus alterum titulum in mūrō cōnspexit:

"Quārtus Holcōniō favet. Holcōnius est candidātus optimus."   25

Quārtus quoque laetissimus erat.

frātrēs Sullae trīgintā dēnāriōs dedērunt. Sulla rīdēbat. postquam Marcus et Quārtus discessērunt, tertium titulum addidit:

MARCVS ET QVARTVS SVNT LIBERALISSIMI

asinus	*ass, donkey*	**intrō īte!**	*go inside!*
senior	*the elder*	**rem cōnfēcit**	*finished the job*
ērāde!	*rub out! erase!*	**tertium**	*third*
īnscrīptiōnem	*writing*	**addidit**	*added*
ērāsit	*rubbed out, erased*	**līberālissimī**	*very generous*
dēsistite!	*stop!*		

About the Language I

A In Stage 9, you met the dative case:

> mercātor **Metellae** togam trādidit.
> *The merchant handed over the toga **to Metella**.*

> Grumiō **hospitibus** cēnam parābat.
> *Grumio was preparing a meal **for the guests**.*

B In Stage 11, you have met some further examples:

> mercātōrēs **agricolīs** respondent.
> *The merchants reply **to the farmers**.*

> Quārtus **Holcōniō** favet.
> *Quartus gives support **to Holconius**.*

> nōs **pistōrī** crēdimus.
> *We give our trust **to the baker**.*

The sentences above can be translated more simply:

> *The merchants answer the farmers.*
> *Quartus supports Holconius.*
> *We trust the baker.*

C Further examples:

1 nōs Āfrō favēmus.
2 vōs amīcīs crēditis.
3 mercātōrēs candidātō nostrō nōn crēdunt.
4 pistōrēs mercātōribus respondent.

D Notice the following use of the dative with the verb **placet**:

> placetne tibi?   mihi placet.
> *Is it pleasing to you?   It is pleasing to me.*

There are more natural ways of translating these examples, such as:

> *Do you like it?   Yes, I do.*
> *Is it okay with you?   Yes, it is.*

E Notice the different cases of the words for *we* and *you (plural)*:

nōs sumus fortēs.
We are brave.

vōs estis ignāvī.
You are lazy.

deī **nōbīs** imperium dant.
The gods give an empire to us.

deī **vōbīs** nihil dant.
The gods give nothing to you.

omnēs **nōs** laudant.
All praise us.

nēmō **vōs** laudat.
No one praises you.

nominative	nōs	vōs
dative	nōbīs	vōbīs
accusative	nōs	vōs

Pompeians listening to a candidate speaking from the steps of the Temple of Jupiter.

Lūcius Spurius Pompōniānus

in vīllā

Grumiō ē culīnā contendit. Clēmēns Grumiōnem videt.

Clēmēns:	babae! togam splendidam geris!
Grumiō:	placetne tibi?
Clēmēns:	mihi placet. quō festīnās, Grumiō?
Grumiō:	ad amphitheātrum contendō. Āfer fautōrēs exspectat. 5
Clēmēns:	num tū Āfrō favēs? Caecilius Holcōniō favet.
Grumiō:	Āfer fautōribus quīnque dēnāriōs prōmīsit. Holcōnius fautōribus duōs dēnāriōs tantum prōmīsit. ego Āfrō faveō, quod vir līberālis est.
Clēmēns:	sed tū servus es. cīvis Pompēiānus nōn es. Āfer cīvibus 10 Pompēiānīs pecūniam prōmīsit.
Grumiō:	Clēmēns, hodiē nōn sum Grumiō. hodiē sum Lūcius Spurius Pompōniānus!
Clēmēns:	Lūcius Spurius Pompōniānus! mendācissimus coquus es! 15
Grumiō:	minimē! hodiē sum pistor Pompēiānus. hodiē nōs pistōrēs ad amphitheātrum convenīmus. nōs Āfrum ad forum dūcimus, ubi cīvēs ōrātiōnēs exspectant. ego ad amphitheātrum contendō. tū mēcum venīs?
Clēmēns:	tēcum veniō. Āfrō nōn faveō. dēnāriōs nōn cupiō, sed 20 dē tē sollicitus sum. rem perīculōsam suscipis. (*exeunt.*)

babae!	*hey!*
quō?	*where?*
fautōrēs	*supporters*
quīnque	*five*
prōmīsit	*promised*
tantum	*only*
mendācissimus	*very deceitful*
ad amphitheātrum	*at the amphitheater*
convenīmus	*gather, meet*
ōrātiōnēs	*speeches*
mēcum	*with me*
dē tē	*about you*
perīculōsam	*dangerous*
suscipis	*you are taking on*
exeunt	*they go out*

prope amphitheātrum

multī pistōrēs ad amphitheātrum conveniunt. Grumiō et Clēmēns ad hanc turbam festīnant.

dīvīsor: festīnāte! festīnāte! nōs Āfrum exspectāmus.
Grumiō: salvē, dīvīsor! ego sum Lūcius Spurius Pompōniānus
                 et hic (*Grumiō Clēmentem pulsat*) servus meus est. ego et   5
                 Āfer amīcissimī sumus.
dīvīsor: ecce quīnque dēnāriī!
                 (*dīvīsor Grumiōnī dēnāriōs dat. dīvīsor Grumiōnī fūstem*
                 quoque trādit.)
Grumiō: Āfer mihi dēnāriōs, nōn fūstem prōmīsit.   10
Clēmēns: Āfer vir līberālis est.
Grumiō: tacē, pessime serve!
dīvīsor: fūstēs ūtilissimī sunt. Holcōnius et amīcī sunt in forō.
pistor: ecce Āfer! Āfer adest!
                 (*Āfer et fautōrēs per viās ad forum contendunt.*)   15

dīvīsor	agent (hired to distribute bribes at elections)
festīnāte!	hurry!
amīcissimī	very friendly, very good friends
tacē!	shut up! be quiet!
ūtilissimī	very useful

in forō

pistōrēs cum Clēmente et cum Grumiōne Āfrum ad forum dūcunt.

pistor prīmus: Pompēiānī Āfrō favent.
pistor secundus: Āfer est melior quam Holcōnius.
pistor tertius: nōs Āfrō crēdimus.
Clēmēns: Grumiō! in forō sunt Holcōnius et amīcī.   5
                        Holcōnium et amīcōs videō.
Grumiō: euge! fēminās videō, ancillās videō, puellās
                        … ēheu! Caecilium videō! Caecilius cum
                        Holcōniō stat! ad vīllam reveniō!
Clēmēns: Grumiō, manē!   10
                        (*Grumiō fugit.*)
mercātor prīmus: Holcōnius est vir nōbilis.
mercātor secundus: Holcōnius melior est quam Āfer.
mercātor tertius: nōs mercātōrēs Holcōniō favēmus.
                        (*pistōrēs et mercātōrēs conveniunt. īrātī sunt.*)   15
pistor prīmus: Holcōnius est asinus. vōs quoque estis
                        asinī, quod Holcōniō crēditis.

mercātor prīmus:	Āfer est caudex. vōs quoque estis caudicēs, quod Āfrō crēditis.
pistor secundus:	amīcī! mercātōrēs nōs "caudicēs" vocant. *20* nōs nōn sumus caudicēs. fortissimī sumus. fūstēs habēmus.
mercātor secundus:	amīcī! pistōrēs nōs "asinōs" vocant. nōs nōn sumus asinī. nōs fortiōrēs sumus quam pistōrēs. magnōs fūstēs habēmus. *25* (*mercātōrēs et pistōrēs in forō pugnant.*)

caudex   *blockhead, idiot*

in culīnā

Clēmēns in culīnā sedet. Grumiō intrat.

Clēmēns:	salvē, Pompōniāne! hercle! toga tua scissa est!
Grumiō:	ēheu! Holcōnius et amīcī in forō mē cēpērunt. postquam fūstem meum cōnspexērunt, clāmābant, "ecce pistor fortis!" tum mercātōrēs mē *5* verberāvērunt. dēnāriōs meōs rapuērunt. nunc nūllōs dēnāriōs habeō.
Clēmēns:	ego decem dēnāriōs habeō!
Grumiō:	decem dēnāriōs?
Clēmēns:	Caecilius mihi decem dēnāriōs dedit, quod servus *10* fidēlis sum. postquam pistōrēs et mercātōrēs pugnam commīsērunt, Caecilius mē cōnspexit. duo pistōrēs Caecilium verberābant. dominus noster auxilium postulābat. Caecilius mēcum ē forō effūgit. dominus noster mihi decem dēnāriōs dedit, quod līberālis est. *15*
Grumiō:	Caecilius est …
Clēmēns:	valē, Pompōniāne!
Grumiō:	quō festīnās, Clēmēns?
Clēmēns:	ad portum festīnō. ibi Poppaea mē exspectat. placetne tibi? *20*
Grumiō:	mihi nōn placet!

scissa	*torn*
rapuērunt	*seized, grabbed*
auxilium	*help*
effūgit	*escaped*

About the Language II

A So far you have met the following ways of asking questions in Latin:

- By means of a question word such as **quis, quid, ubi, cūr**:

quis est Quīntus?	*Who is Quintus?*
quid tū facis?	*What are you doing?*
ubi est ānulus?	*Where is the ring?*
cūr tū lacrimās?	*Why are you crying?*

- By tone of voice, indicated in writing by a question mark:

tū pecūniam dēbēs?	*Do you owe money?*
tū ānulum habēs?	*Do you have the ring?*

- By adding **-ne** to the first word of the sentence:

vōsne estis contentī?	*Are you satisfied?*
placetne tibi?	*Does it please you?*

- By means of the question word **num**. This word is used to suggest that the answer to the question will be *no*. Notice the different ways of translating it:

num Quīntus timet?	*Surely Quintus is not afraid?*
	Quintus is not afraid, is he?
num tū Āfrō favēs?	*Surely you don't support Afer?*
	You don't support Afer, do you?

B Further examples:

1 cūr tū in hortō labōrās?
2 quis est āthlēta ille?
3 tū discum habēs?
4 vōsne estis īrātī?
5 ubi sunt mercātōrēs?
6 quid quaeris, domina?
7 tūne Pompēiānus es?
8 quis vīnum portat?
9 cēnam parās?
10 num cēnam parās?

Practicing the Language

A Complete each sentence with the correct word from the box below. Then translate the sentence. Do not use any word more than once.

> contendō   faveō
> contendis   favēs
> contendimus   favēmus
> contenditis   favētis

1 ego ad forum . . . . . ego sum candidātus.
2 tū Āfrō . . . . . tū es stultus.
3 ego Holcōniō . . . . ., quod Holcōnius est candidātus optimus.
4 nōs Holcōniō nōn . . . . ., quod Holcōnius est asinus.
5 Clēmēns, cūr tū ad portum . . . . ?
6 vōs Āfrō . . . . , quod vōs estis pistōrēs.
7 nōs ad vīllam . . . . ., quod in forō sunt Holcōnius et amīcī.
8 ēheu! cūr ē forō . . . . ? vōs dēnāriōs meōs habētis!

B Complete each sentence with the correct form of the noun. Then translate the sentence.

1 Quārtus Sullae decem dēnāriōs dedit. Sulla (titulus, titulum) in mūrō scrīpsit.
2 fūr thermās intrābat. (mercātor, mercātōrem) eum agnōvit.
3 multī candidātī sunt in forō. ego (Holcōnius, Holcōnium) videō.
4 ego ad portum currō. (ancilla, ancillae) mē exspectat.
5 hodiē ad urbem contendō. in amphitheātrō sunt (leō, leōnēs).
6 rhētor est īrātus. rhētor (puerī, puerōs) exspectat.
7 fēminae sunt in tabernā. mercātōrēs fēminīs (stolae, stolās) ostendunt.
8 postquam Holcōnius et amīcī Grumiōnem cēpērunt, quīnque (dēnāriī, dēnāriōs) rapuērunt.

C Refer to the stories **Marcus et Quārtus** and **Sulla** on pages 184–5. Then select the correct word from the box below and translate each sentence. Do not use any word more than once.

Āfrō	mihi
candidātīs	nōbīs
frātrī	scrīptōrī
frātribus	tibi
Holcōniō	vōbīs

1 Marcus . . . . favet, quod candidātus dīves est.
2 "minimē!" Quārtus . . . . respondit. "vir nōbilis melior est quam vir dīves. . . . . crēdō."
3 frātrēs dissentiēbant. Quārtus, postquam Sullam quaesīvit, ... decem dēnāriōs dedit.
4 Sulla Marcō titulum ostendit. "placetne . . . . ?" rogāvit Sulla.
5 " . . . . nōn placet," respondit Marcus.
6 Sulla titulōs aliōs in mūrō scrīpsit. hī titulī . . . . Āfrō et Holcōniō, favērunt.
7 Sulla . . . . titulōs ostendit. "placetne . . . . ?"
8 "placet . . . . !" clāmāvērunt Marcus et Quārtus.

Candidates also made speeches from a special platform in the forum.

Local Government and Elections

The Pompeians took local politics seriously, and the annual elections, which were held at the end of March, were very lively. As soon as the names of candidates were published, election fever gripped the town. Slogans appeared on the walls; groups of **fautōrēs** (supporters) held processions through the streets, and the candidates spoke at public meetings in the forum.

Every year, two pairs of officials were elected by the people. The senior pair, called **duovirī**, were responsible for hearing evidence and giving judgment in court. The other pair, called **aedīlēs**, had the task of supervising the public markets, the police force, the baths, the places of public entertainment, the water supply, and the sewers. It was their duty to see that the public services were efficiently run and the local taxes spent wisely.

In addition to these four officials, there was a town council of one hundred leading citizens, most of whom had already served as duoviri or aediles. New members were chosen not by the people but by the council itself.

This building was used as the meeting place of the town council.

The public officials might provide free bread for the poor. One election slogan recommends a candidate who "brings good bread."

A candidate himself wore a toga, specially whitened with chalk, in order to be easily recognized. The word **candidātus** is connected with **candidus** which means "dazzling white." The candidates, attended by their clients, walked around greeting voters while their agents praised their qualities, made promises on their behalf, and distributed bribes in the form of money. This financial bribery was illegal but was widely practiced. Legal forms of persuasion included promises of games and entertainments if the candidate won. In fact, it was expected that those who were elected would show their gratitude to the voters by putting on splendid shows in the theater and amphitheater at their own expense.

A successful candidate would also be expected to contribute from his own wealth to the construction or repair of public buildings. The family of the Holconii, whose names often appear in the lists of Pompeian duoviri and aediles, were connected with the building of the large theater, and another wealthy family, the Flacci, helped to pay for other civic buildings. The Flacci also had a reputation for putting on excellent entertainments.

This tradition of public service, encouraged by the emperors, was an important part of Roman public life and made it possible for a small town like Pompeii to enjoy benefits which could not have been paid for by local taxes alone. It also meant that men who wanted to take part in the government of their town had to be wealthy. They came from two groups: a small core of wealthy families, like the Holconii, whose members were regularly elected to the most important offices and a larger, less powerful group which changed frequently.

Although public service was unpaid and was not a means of making money, it gave a man a position of importance in his town. The wide seats in the front row of the theater, which gave a close-up view of the chorus and actors, were reserved for him; he also had a special place close to the arena in the amphitheater. In due course the town council might erect a statue to him, and he would have his name inscribed on any building to whose construction or repair he had contributed. The Romans were not modest people. They were eager for honor and fame among their fellow citizens. There was, therefore, no shortage of candidates to compete for these rewards at election time.

Caecilius does not seem to have stood as a candidate, although in many ways he was an outstanding citizen and had made a considerable fortune. Perhaps he preferred to concentrate on his business activities and was content to support candidates from the great political families like the Holconii.

Pompeii was free to run its own affairs, but, if the local officials were unable to preserve law and order, the central government at Rome might take over and run the town. This actually happened after the famous riot in A.D. 59 described in Stage 8, when many people were killed or wounded after the Nucerians quarreled with the Pompeians at a gladiatorial show given by Livineius Regulus. The Nucerians complained to Emperor Nero; Regulus himself was sent into exile, and games in Pompeii were banned for ten years. In the following year, A.D. 60, Nero dismissed the duoviri and appointed a special officer or **praefectus** to run the affairs of the town. This was a strong sign of official disapproval, and two years passed before the local people were again trusted to take care of themselves.

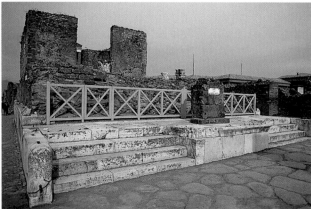

We know that the Temple of Fortuna Augusta, situated just to the north of the forum, was built largely by the generosity of Marcus Tullius who owned the whole of the site on which it was built.

The town council might erect a statue to a leading politician. This is M. Holconius Rufus (also seen on page 181).

Election Notices

Many of the thousands of graffiti found in Pompeii refer to the elections held there in March A.D. 79. Here are two of them:

> **Casellius for aedile.**
> **We want Titus Claudius Verus for duovir.**

Political supporters represented all kinds of people and interests.

Sometimes they were groups of neighbors, **vīcīnī**, who lived in the same area as the candidate. They would certainly include the candidate's personal friends and his clients. Sometimes, however, appeals were made to particular trade groups. One notice reads:

Innkeepers, vote for Sallustius Capito!

Others were addressed to barbers, mule-drivers, pack-carriers, bakers, and fishermen. It is thought that most of the slogans were organized by the agents of the candidates and groups of their supporters rather than by private individuals.

This method of electioneering by wall slogans naturally invited replies by rival supporters. One candidate, Vatia, was made to look ridiculous by this comment:

All the people who are fast asleep vote for Vatia.

Pompeian women did not have the right to vote or hold office. Only adult male citizens were allowed to cast votes in the **comitium** (the permanent voting hall in the forum) on election day. Nevertheless, women took a lively interest in local politics, had considerable influence, and supported the various candidates vigorously. There are, for example, several slogans written by the girls who worked in a bar belonging to a woman called Asellina.

This notice reads: "Vote for Gnaeus Helvius Sabinus as aedile. He deserves public office."

It appears that these notices were often painted on the walls at night by lantern light, either because the streets were then more or less deserted and so there was less risk of trouble from rival supporters, or because it was easier at night to put up a ladder for an hour or two without causing congestion on the sidewalks.

At top right there is part of a notice advertising a fight of ten pairs of gladiators. It may have been paid for by a candidate in the elections.

Word Study

A Match each word to its correct definition listed below:

liberal	rapacious	stultify
mural	reverberate	utilitarian
placate	solicitous	

1 . . . . . a wall-painting or drawing
2 . . . . . to cause to appear foolish
3 . . . . . practical, functional
4 . . . . . to soothe or pacify
5 . . . . . anxious, concerned, eager
6 . . . . . taking by force, avaricious
7 . . . . . generous; free-thinking
8 . . . . . to echo, resound

B Read the following sentences, and place the correct words in the blanks:

| credible | incredulous | valor |
| genteel | surreptitious | |

"Pomponianus" used Clemens as his slave to present himself as a more . . . . citizen. He also tried to affect a more sophisticated and . . . . manner. Grumio had taken Caecilius' toga in a . . . . way, since the master was away, but it was Clemens who showed real . . . . during the brawl. Later Grumio was . . . . that Clemens was rewarded.

C Give the Latin root from which these words are derived:

1 virtue
2 convenient
3 valiant
4 creed
5 legible
6 complacent
7 rapt
8 primitive

Stage 11
Vocabulary Checklist

convenit: convēnit	*gathers, meets*
crēdit: crēdidit (+ DAT)	*trusts, believes, has faith in*
dē	*down from; about*
favet: fāvit (+ DAT)	*favors, supports*
gēns: gentem	*family*
invītat: invītāvit	*invites*
legit: lēgit	*reads*
līberālis	*generous*
minimē!	*no!*
mūrus	*wall*
noster: nostrum	*our*
nunc	*now*
placet: placuit (+ DAT)	*it pleases, suits*
prīmus	*first*
prōmittit: prōmīsit	*promises*
pugna	*fight*
rapit: rapuit	*seizes, grabs*
secundus	*second*
senātor: senātōrem	*senator*
sollicitus	*worried, anxious*
stultus	*stupid*
tertius	*third*
ūtilis	*useful*
valē!	*good-bye!*
verberat: verberāvit	*strikes, beats*
vir: virum	*man*

L. Ceius Secundus is proposed for aedile.

VESUVIUS

Stage 12

mōns īrātus

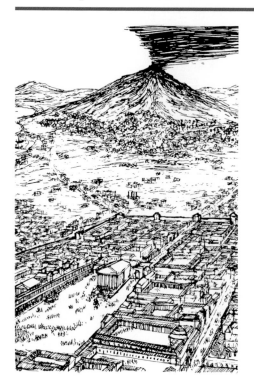

1 Syphāx et Celer in portū stābant.
  amīcī montem spectābant.

2 Syphāx amīcō dīxit,
  "ego prope portum servōs
  vēndēbam. ego subitō sonōs
  audīvī."

3 Celer Syphācī respondit,
  "tū sonōs audīvistī. ego
  tremōrēs sēnsī. ego prope
  montem ambulābam."

4 Poppaea et Lucriō in ātriō
stābant. sollicitī erant.

5 Poppaea Lucriōnī dīxit,
"ego in forō eram. ego tibi
togam quaerēbam. ego
nūbem mīrābilem
cōnspexī."

6 Lucriō Poppaeae respondit,
"tū nūbem cōnspexistī. ego
cinerem sēnsī. ego flammās
vīdī."

7 Marcus et Quārtus in forō
erant. Sulla ad frātrēs
contendit.

8 Sulla frātribus dīxit,
"ego ad theātrum
contendēbam.
ego sonōs audīvī et tremōrēs
sēnsī. vōs sonōs audīvistis?
vōs tremōrēs sēnsistis?"

9 frātrēs Sullae respondērunt,
"nōs tremōrēs sēnsimus et
sonōs audīvimus.
nōs nūbem mīrābilem
vīdimus. nōs sollicitī
sumus."

The Terrible Mountain

Right: A Pompeian painting of Vesuvius as Caecilius knew it, with vineyards on its fertile slopes.

Below: This is what Vesuvius might have looked like when it erupted in A.D. 79; steam rising in the crater today; and the view from the sea, with the central cone replaced by two lower summits.

tremōrēs

When you have read this story, answer the questions opposite.

Caecilius cum Iūliō cēnābat. Iūlius in vīllā splendidā prope Nūceriam habitābat.

Iūlius Caeciliō dīxit, "ego sollicitus sum. ego in hortō heri ambulābam et librum legēbam. subitō terra valdē tremuit. ego tremōrēs sēnsī. quid tū agēbās?" 5

"ego servō epistulās dictābam," inquit Caecilius. "ego quoque tremōrēs sēnsī. postquam terra tremuit, Grumiō tablīnum intrāvit et mē ad hortum dūxit. nōs nūbem mīrābilem vīdimus."

"vōs timēbātis?" rogāvit Iūlius.

"nōs nōn timēbāmus," Caecilius Iūliō respondit. "ego, 10 postquam nūbem cōnspexī, familiam meam ad larārium vocāvī. tum nōs laribus sacrificium fēcimus."

"hercle! vōs fortissimī erātis," clāmāvit Iūlius. "vōs tremōrēs sēnsistis, vōs nūbem cōnspexistis. vōs tamen nōn erātis perterritī."

"nōs nōn timēbāmus, quod nōs laribus crēdēbāmus," inquit 15 Caecilius. "iamprīdem terra tremuit. iamprīdem tremōrēs vīllās et mūrōs dēlēvērunt. sed larēs vīllam meam et familiam meam servāvērunt. ego igitur sollicitus nōn sum."

subitō servus triclīnium intrāvit.

"domine, Clēmēns est in ātriō. Clēmēns ex urbe vēnit. 20 Caecilium quaerit," servus Iūliō dīxit.

"nōn intellegō," Caecilius exclāmāvit. "ego Clēmentem ad fundum meum māne mīsī."

servus Clēmentem in triclīnium dūxit.

"cūr tū ē fundō discessistī? cūr tū ad hanc vīllam vēnistī?" 25 rogāvit Caecilius.

Clēmēns dominō et Iūliō rem tōtam nārrāvit.

tremōrēs	*tremors*	**nūbem**	*cloud*
cum Iūliō	*with Julius*	**familiam**	*household*
tremuit	*shook*	**larārium**	*domestic shrine*
sēnsī	*felt*	**laribus**	*household gods*
agēbās	*were doing*	**sacrificium**	*sacrifice*
epistulās	*letters*	**iamprīdem**	*a long time ago*
dictābam	*was dictating*	**fundum**	*farm*

Questions

1 What was Caecilius doing at the beginning of this story? Where was he?
2 What had Julius been doing the day before? Why was he now worried?
3 What had Caecilius been doing when the tremors began?
4 What did Caecilius say that he and Grumio had seen when they went into the garden?
5 What two things did Caecilius say he had done next (lines 11–12)?
6 Why did Julius think that Caecilius and his household were **fortissimī** (lines 13–14)?
7 Why was Caecilius so sure that his Lares (gods) would look after his household (lines 16–18)?
8 **subitō servus triclīnium intrāvit** (line 19). What news did he bring?
9 What was Caecilius' reaction to the news? Why did he react in this way?
10 Read the last three lines of the story. Why do you think Clemens has come?

At the time of the eruption, Caecilius' lararium was decorated with marble pictures of the earthquake that happened in A.D. 62.

This is how Caecilius would have pictured a Lar, one of the gods who guarded his household.

ad urbem

"ego ad fundum tuum contendī," Clēmēns dominō dīxit. "ego vīlicō epistulam tuam trādidī. postquam vīlicus epistulam lēgit, nōs fundum et servōs īnspiciēbāmus. subitō nōs ingentēs sonōs audīvimus. nōs tremōrēs quoque sēnsimus. tum ego montem spectāvī et nūbem mīrābilem vīdī." 5

"quid vōs fēcistis?" rogāvit Iūlius.

"nōs urbem petīvimus, quod valdē timēbāmus," respondit Clēmēns. "ego, postquam urbem intrāvī, clāmōrem ingentem audīvī. multī Pompēiānī per viās currēbant. fēminae cum īnfantibus per urbem festīnābant. fīliī et fīliae parentēs quaerēbant. 10 ego ad vīllam nostram pervēnī, ubi Metella et Quīntus manēbant. Quīntus mē ad tē mīsit, quod nōs omnēs perterritī erāmus."

Caecilius ad urbem contendit, quod sollicitus erat. Iūlius et Clēmēns quoque ad urbem festīnāvērunt. maxima turba viās complēbat, quod Pompēiānī ē vīllīs festīnābant. 15

prope urbem Holcōnium cōnspexērunt. Holcōnius cum servīs ad portum fugiēbat.

"cūr vōs ad urbem contenditis? cūr nōn ad portum fugitis?" rogāvit Holcōnius.

"ad vīllam meam contendō," Caecilius Holcōniō respondit. 20 "Metellam et Quīntum quaerō. tū Metellam vīdistī? Quīntum cōnspexistī?"

"ēheu!" clāmāvit Holcōnius. "ego vīllam splendidam habēbam. in vīllā erant statuae pulchrae et pictūrae pretiōsae. iste mōns vīllam meam dēlēvit; omnēs statuae sunt frāctae." 25

"sed, amīce, tū uxōrem meam vīdistī?" rogāvit Caecilius.

"ego nihil dē Metellā sciō. nihil cūrō," respondit Holcōnius.

"furcifer!" clāmāvit Caecilius. "tū vīllam tuam āmīsistī. ego uxōrem meam āmīsī!"

Caecilius, postquam Holcōnium vituperāvit, ad urbem 30 contendit.

vīlicō	*farm manager*	pretiōsae	*precious*
sonōs	*noises*	iste mōns	*that (terrible) mountain*
fīliae	*daughters*	sciō	*know*
parentēs	*parents*	nihil cūrō	*I don't care*
pervēnī	*reached, arrived at*		

ad vīllam

in urbe pavor maximus erat. cinis iam dēnsior incidēbat. flammae
ubīque erant. Caecilius et amīcī, postquam urbem intrāvērunt,
vīllam petēbant. sed iter erat difficile, quod multī Pompēiānī viās
complēbant. Caecilius tamen per viās fortiter contendēbat.

nūbēs iam dēnsissima erat. subitō Iūlius exclāmāvit,   5
"vōs ad vīllam contendite! ego nōn valeō."

statim ad terram dēcidit exanimātus. Clēmēns Iūlium ad
templum proximum portāvit.

"tū optimē fēcistī," Caecilius servō dīxit. "tū Iūlium servāvistī.
ego tibi lībertātem prōmittō."   10

tum Caecilius ē templō discessit et ad vīllam cucurrit.

Clēmēns cum Iūliō in templō manēbat. tandem Iūlius respīrāvit.
"ubi sumus?" rogāvit.

"sumus tūtī," servus Iūliō respondit. "dea Īsis nōs servāvit.
postquam tū in terram dēcidistī, ego tē ad hoc templum portāvī."   15

"tibi grātiās maximās agō, quod tū mē servāvistī," inquit Iūlius.
"sed ubi est Caecilius?"

"dominus meus ad vīllam contendit," respondit Clēmēns.

"ēheu! stultissimus est Caecilius!" clāmāvit Iūlius. "sine dubiō
Metella et Quīntus mortuī sunt. ego ex urbe quam celerrimē   20
discēdō. tū mēcum venīs?"

"minimē, amīce!" Clēmēns Iūliō respondit. "ego dominum
meum quaerō!"

pavor	panic	Īsis	Isis (Great Mother goddess of Egypt)
cinis	ash	sine dubiō	without a doubt
iam	now		
dēnsior	thicker		
incidēbat	was falling		
flammae	flames		
iter	journey, progress		
difficile	difficult		
valeō	feel well		
exanimātus	unconscious		
templum	temple		
proximum	nearest		
lībertātem	freedom		
respīrāvit	recovered consciousness, revived		
tūtī	safe		
dea	goddess		

The goddess Isis, on a ring.

fīnis

iam nūbēs ātra ad terram dēscendēbat; iam cinis dēnsissimus incidēbat. plūrimī Pompēiānī iam dē urbe suā dēspērābant. multī perībant. Clēmēns tamen nōn dēspērābat, sed obstinātē vīllam petīvit, quod Caecilium quaerēbat. tandem ad vīllam pervēnit. sollicitus ruīnās spectāvit. tōta vīlla ardēbat. Clēmēns fūmum 5 ubīque vīdit. per ruīnās tamen fortiter contendit et dominum suum vocāvit. Caecilius tamen nōn respondit. subitō canis lātrāvit. servus tablīnum intrāvit, ubi canis erat. Cerberus dominum custōdiēbat.

Caecilius in tablīnō moribundus iacēbat. mūrus sēmirutus eum 10 paene cēlābat. Clēmēns dominō vīnum dedit. Caecilius, postquam vīnum bibit, sēnsim respīrāvit.

"quid accidit, domine?" rogāvit Clēmēns.

"ego ad vīllam vēnī," inquit Caecilius. "Metellam nōn vīdī! Quīntum nōn vīdī! vīlla erat dēserta. tum ego ad tablīnum 15 contendēbam. subitō terra tremuit et pariēs in mē incidit. tū es servus fidēlis. abī! ego tē iubeō. dē vītā meā dēspērō. Metella et Quīntus periērunt. nunc ego quoque sum moritūrus."

Clēmēns recūsāvit. in tablīnō obstinātē manēbat. Caecilius iterum clāmāvit: 20

"Clēmēns, abī! tē iubeō. fortasse Quīntus superfuit. quaere Quīntum! hunc ānulum Quīntō dā!"

Caecilius, postquam Clēmentī ānulum suum trādidit, statim exspīrāvit. Clēmēns dominō trīste valedīxit et ē vīllā discessit.

Cerberus tamen in vīllā mānsit. dominum frūstrā custōdiēbat. 25

fīnis	end	accidit	happened
ātra	black	pariēs	wall
dēscendēbat	was coming down	iubeō	order
plūrimī	most	periērunt	have died,
perībant	were dying,		have perished
	were perishing	moritūrus	going to die
obstinātē	stubbornly	recūsāvit	refused
ruīnās	ruins, wreckage	superfuit	has survived
fūmum	smoke	exspīrāvit	died
moribundus	almost dead	trīste	sadly
sēmirutus	half-collapsed	valedīxit	said good-bye
sēnsim	slowly, gradually		

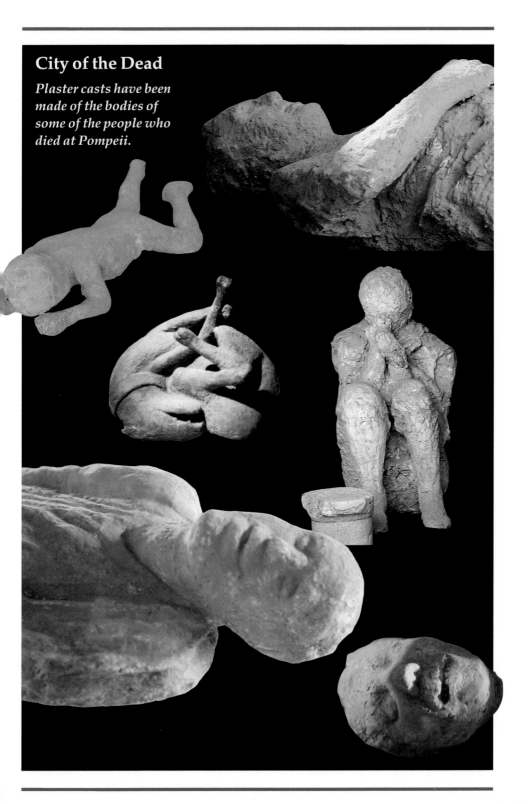

City of the Dead

Plaster casts have been made of the bodies of some of the people who died at Pompeii.

About the Language

A In Stage 6 you met the imperfect and perfect tenses:

IMPERFECT		PERFECT	
portābat	*s/he was carrying*	portāvit	*s/he carried*
portābant	*they were carrying*	portāvērunt	*they carried*

B In Stage 12, you have met the imperfect and perfect tenses with *I*, *you*, and *we* :

IMPERFECT		PERFECT	
(ego) portābam	*I was carrying*	(ego) portāvī	*I carried*
(tū) portābās	*you (singular) were carrying*	(tū) portāvistī	*you (sing.) carried*
(nōs) portābāmus	*we were carrying*	(nōs) portāvimus	*we carried*
(vōs) portābātis	*you (plural) were carrying*	(vōs) portāvistis	*you (plural) carried*

ego, tū, nōs , and **vōs** are used only for emphasis and are usually left out.

C The full imperfect and perfect tenses are:

IMPERFECT		PERFECT	
(ego)	portābam	(ego)	portāvī
(tū)	portābās	(tū)	portāvistī
	portābat		portāvit
(nōs)	portābāmus	(nōs)	portāvimus
(vōs)	portābātis	(vōs)	portāvistis
	portābant		portāvērunt

D The full imperfect tense of **sum** is:

(ego)	eram	*I was*
(tū)	erās	*you (singular) were*
	erat	*s/he was*
(nōs)	erāmus	*we were*
(vōs)	erātis	*you (plural) were*
	erant	*they were*

E Further examples:

1 portāvistis; portābātis; portābāmus
2 trāxī; trāxērunt; trāxistī
3 docēbant; docuī; docuimus
4 erātis; audīvī; trahēbam

The Temple of Isis, Pompeii.

Practicing the Language

A Select the correct verb and then translate each sentence.

1 **a** Iūlius Caecilium rogāvit, "(audīvistīne, audīvistisne) sonōs?"

    b Caecilius Iūliō respondit, "sonōs (audīvī, audivīmus)."

2 **a** "Marce! Quārte! num in vīllā (mānsistī, mānsistis)?"

    b "minimē! in vīllā nōn (mānsī, mānsimus)," clāmāvērunt Marcus et Quārtus.

3 **a** Caecilius amīcōs rogāvit: "(vīdistīne, vīdistisne) Metellam?"

    b "Metellam nōn (cōnspexī, cōnspeximus)," respondērunt amīcī.

B Translate the following questions, and then select and translate the appropriate answer for the particular question.

1 **quid tū sēnsistī?**
    a ego tremōrēs sēnsī.
    b nōs tremōrēs sēnsimus.
    c vōs tremōrēs sēnsistis.

2 **vōsne timēbātis?**
    a ego nōn timēbam.
    b tū nōn timēbās.
    c nōs nōn timēbāmus.

3 **quid tū āmīsistī?**
    a ego pictūram pretiōsam āmīsī.
    b tū pictūram pretiōsam āmīsistī.
    c nōs pictūram pretiōsam āmīsimus.

4 **cūr vōs ex urbe festīnāvistis?**
    a ego festīnāvī quod perterritus eram.
    b tū festīnāvistī quod perterritus erās.
    c nōs festīnāvimus quod perterritī erāmus.

5 **vōsne ad portum contendēbātis?**
    a tū ad portum contendēbās.
    b nōs ad portum contendēbāmus.
    c vōs ad portum contendēbātis.

C Select the correct form of the noun in parentheses, and then translate the sentence.

1 nūbem mīrābilem spectābāmus sed nōn timēbāmus. (laribus, larēs) sacrificium fēcimus.
2 Iūlius, postquam in templō respīrāvit, (Clēmentī, Clēmentem) grātiās ēgit.
3 Clēmēns Iūliō (viae, viam) ostendit.
4 Caecilius, postquam Holcōnius dē Metellā nihil cūrāvit, (Holcōniō, Holcōnium) nōn fāvit.
5 Holcōnius cum servīs ex urbe fugiēbat. "prōmittitne dominus (nōbīs, nōs) lībertātem?" servī sibi dīxērunt.
6 "minimē! Holcōnius dē vīllā cūrat. (vōbīs, vōs) lībertātem nōn offert."

Vesuvius erupting in the eighteenth century.

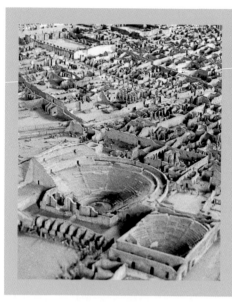

Above: **The area covered by ash from the eruption.** *Left:* **Ash covered the city to the height of the walls shown in this model of the excavations. The theaters are in the foreground.**

The Destruction and Excavation of Pompeii

On the night of August 23–24 A.D. 79, it rained hard; a strong wind blew, and earth tremors were felt. During the following morning, Vesuvius, which had been an inactive volcano for many centuries, erupted with enormous violence, devastating much of the surrounding area. A huge mass of mud poured down the mountainside and swallowed the town of Herculaneum; hot stones and ash descended in vast quantities on Pompeii, burying everything to a depth of fifteen to twenty feet (four-and-a-half to six meters). Most people, with vivid memories of the earthquake of seventeen years before, fled into the open countryside carrying a few possessions, but others remained behind, hoping that the storm would pass. They died, buried in the ruins of their homes or suffocated by sulfur fumes.

By the end of two days, the whole of Pompeii was a desert of white ash. Here and there the tops of buildings could be seen, and little groups of survivors struggled back to salvage what they could. They dug tunnels to get down to their homes and rescue money, furniture, and other valuables. But nothing could be done to excavate and rebuild the town itself. The site was abandoned; thousands of refugees made new homes in Naples and other Campanian towns. Gradually the ruins collapsed, a new layer of soil covered the site, and Pompeii disappeared from view.

During the Middle Ages, nobody knew exactly where the town lay. Only a vague memory survived in the name "civita" (Italian for "city") by which the local people still called the low hill. But what city it was or whether there really was a city buried there, they neither knew nor cared.

Left: Herculaneum. In the foreground are some of the excavated Roman buildings. The modern buildings in the distance lie above the unexcavated part of the town. The second floor of houses survives here. Below: A table is still in place in an upper room.

Uncovering the Temple of Isis in 1765.

The Rediscovery of Pompeii and Herculaneum

The first remains of Pompeii were found in 1594, when an Italian architect named Fontana was constructing a water channel from the River Sarno to a nearby town. He discovered the remains of buildings and an inscription. But these were misunderstood as it was thought that a villa belonging to the famous Roman politician, Pompeius, had been discovered. Nothing much was done for another 150 years, until in 1748, Charles III, King of Naples, began to excavate the site in search of treasure. In 1763, the treasure seekers realized they were exploring the lost city of Pompeii. At Herculaneum the excavations were much more difficult because the volcanic mud had turned to hard rock, and the town lay up to forty feet (twelve meters) below the new ground level. Tunneling down was slow and dangerous work.

In the early days of excavation, no effort was made to uncover the sites in an orderly way; the methods of modern archaeology were unknown. The excavators were not interested in uncovering towns in order to learn about the people who had lived there but were looking for jewelry, statues, and other works of art, which were then taken away to decorate the palaces of kings and rich men.

At the beginning of the nineteenth century, however, the looting was stopped, and systematic excavation began. Section by section, the soil and rubble were cleared. The most fragile and precious objects were taken to the National Museum in Naples, but everything else was kept where it was found. As buildings were uncovered, they were partly reconstructed with original materials to preserve them and make them safe for visitors.

From time to time, archaeologists found a hollow space in the solidified ash where an object of wood or other organic material had perished. To find out what it was, they poured liquid plaster into the hole, and, when it hardened, they carefully removed the surrounding ash and were left with a perfect image of the original object. This work still continues, but now resin is used instead of plaster. In this way many wooden doors and shutters have been discovered as well as bodies of human beings and animals.

A resin cast of a young woman's body. Unlike plaster, resin is transparent and bones and jewelry can be seen through it. Resin is also less fragile than plaster.

Nowadays every bone and object discovered is carefully examined, recorded and conserved. This skeleton was discovered at Herculaneum in 1982. The bones showed that she was a woman of about 45, with a protruding jaw; she had gum disease but no cavities in her teeth. Her wealth was clear from her rings and the bracelets and earrings (below) that had been in her purse. By contrast, the bones of slaves may show signs of overwork and undernourishment.

At Herculaneum, where the town was hermetically sealed by the solidified mud, perishable objects, such as wooden doors and stairs, woven material, fishermen's nets, and wax tablets, have survived intact.

The work is not yet finished. Only about three-fifths of Pompeii have so far been uncovered and less of Herculaneum. Whenever a new house is opened up, the archaeologists find it just as it was abandoned. They may discover the remains of a meal, pots on the stove, coins in the tablinum, lampstands in various rooms, wall-paintings (often only slightly damaged), the lead pipes which supplied water to the fountains in the garden, brooches, needles, jars of cosmetics, shoes, and toys; in fact, all the hundreds of small things that went to make up a Roman home. If they are lucky, they may also discover the name of the family that lived there.

Thus, through the efforts of archaeologists, a remarkably detailed picture of the life of this ordinary Roman town has emerged from the disaster which destroyed it 2,000 years ago.

The People Died – the Garden Lives

Above: Plaster casts are also made of tree-roots, which help identify the trees planted in the gardens and orchards of Pompeii. The position of each vine in this vineyard was identified, and it has now been replanted. Right: In the corner of the vineyard, just inside the city wall, huddles a group of adults and children that failed to get away.

Word Study

A From the list match each word to its meaning using the underlined words as cues:

adjacent   inter   peninsula
epistle   intimidate   refugee
incinerate

1 to reduce to <u>ashes</u>
2 <u>lying</u> next to, adjoining
3 one of the <u>letters</u> of the New Testament
4 to cause <u>fear</u>
5 geographic structure which is <u>almost</u> an island
6 one <u>fleeing</u> to a safe haven
7 to place a body <u>in the ground</u>

B Match these derivatives of **sentit** to their definitions.

1 sentient   **a** conscious, having sense perception
2 sensuous   **b** agreement
3 sensual   **c** disagreement
4 presentiment   **d** pithy, filled with aphorisms
5 sententious   **e** given to gratification of the senses
6 dissent   **f** appealing to the senses
7 consensus   **g** a premonition

C Match the word to its definition.

1 paramount   **a** an expression of praise or congratulation
2 tantamount   **b** of chief concern, foremost
3 permissive   **c** something that completes; parts making up
                     a whole
4 flamboyant   **d** an evasive tactic
5 complement   **e** equivalent in effect or value
6 compliment   **f** lenient, tolerant
7 subterfuge   **g** highly ornate, overwrought

Stage 12
Vocabulary Checklist

āmittit: āmīsit	*loses*
cinis: cinerem	*ash*
complet: complēvit	*fills*
custōdit: custōdīvit	*guards*
dēnsus	*thick*
epistula	*letter*
flamma	*flame*
fortiter	*bravely*
frūstrā	*in vain*
fugit: fūgit	*runs away, flees*
fundus	*farm*
iacet: iacuit	*lies*
iam	*now*
igitur	*therefore*
incidit: incidit	*falls*
mīrābilis	*marvelous, strange, wonderful*
mittit: mīsit	*sends*
mōns: montem	*mountain*
nūbēs: nūbem	*cloud*
optimē	*very well*
paene	*nearly, almost*
sentit: sēnsit	*feels*
tandem	*at last*
templum	*temple*
terra	*ground, land*
timet: timuit	*is afraid, fears*

You have also met the following numbers:

ūnus	*one*
duo	*two*
trēs	*three*

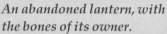

An abandoned lantern, with the bones of its owner.

LANGUAGE
INFORMATION

Contents

About the Language

Nouns

A Words like **puella**, **servus**, **mercātor**, and **leō**, that indicate people, places, or things, are known as **nouns**. In Latin, nouns change their endings according to their function in a sentence (e.g. whether they are subjects or objects of a verb, etc.). These different forms of the same noun are called **cases**. Latin nouns belong to families called **declensions**. Each declension has its own set of endings for the various cases.

B In Unit 1, you have met three cases and three declensions:

	first declension	*second declension*	*third declension*	
SINGULAR				
nominative	puella	servus	mercātor	leō
dative	puellae	servō	mercātōrī	leōnī
accusative	puellam	servum	mercātōrem	leōnem
PLURAL				
nominative	puellae	servī	mercātōrēs	leōnēs
dative	puellīs	servīs	mercātōribus	leōnibus
accusative	puellās	servōs	mercātōrēs	leōnēs

C Review the way the cases are used:

The **nominative case** is used for the subject (whoever/whatever does the action of the verb):

| **mercātor** cantābat. | *The **merchant** was singing.* |
| **servī** labōrābant. | *The **slaves** were working.* |

The nominative case is also used for nouns which complete the verb **est**, since they refer back to the subject:

| Metella est **māter**. | *Metella is the **mother**.* |
| Grumiō et Clēmēns sunt **servī**. | *Grumio and Clemens are **slaves**.* |

The **dative case** indicates the indirect object of a verb, often translated into English by a phrase which begins with the preposition **to** or the preposition **for**, expressed or understood:

> senex **mercātōrī** pictūram ostendit.
> *The old man showed the painting **to the merchant**.*
> or
> *The old man showed **the merchant** the painting.*

> lībertī **puellīs** vīnum ferēbant.
> *The freedmen brought wine **for the girls**.*

Some Latin verbs are always completed by a noun in the dative case, even when the English equivalent does not seem to include **to** or **for**:

> cīvēs **mercātōrī** crēdunt.   *The citizens trust the **merchant**.*
> pistōrēs **Āfrō** favent.   *The bakers support **Afer**.*

The **accusative case** is used for the direct object (whoever/whatever receives the action of a verb):

> Grumiō **puellam** salūtāvit.   *Grumio greeted the **girl**.*
> Caecilius **servōs** vituperāvit.   *Caecilius cursed the **slaves**.*

D In each pair of sentences below, the first sentence contains a noun in the nominative singular (in bold print). Translate that sentence. Then complete the second Latin sentence by writing the correct plural form of the noun in the nominative case. Translate the completed sentence.

> For example: **canis** in viā lātrāvit.
>   *The dog barked in the street.*
> This becomes: **canēs** in viā lātrāvērunt.
>   *The dogs barked in the street.*

1 **servus** dominum timēbat.
    ..... dominum timēbant.

2 **lībertus** in lectō recubuit.
    ..... in lectō recubuērunt.

3 **poēta** versum recitābat.
    ..... versum recitābant.

4 **hospes** vīllam intrāvit.
    ..... vīllam intrāvērunt.

5 Sorex erat **āctor**.
    Sorex et Actius erant ......

E In each pair of sentences below, the first sentence contains a noun in the nominative plural (in bold print). Translate that sentence. Then complete the second Latin sentence by writing the correct singular form of the noun in the nominative case. Translate the completed sentence.

> For example: **mātrēs** līberōs quaerēbant.
> *Mothers were searching for their children.*
> This becomes: **māter** līberōs quaerēbat.
> *The mother was searching for her children.*

1 **agricolae** in viā clāmābant.
..... in viā clāmābat.

2 **fūrēs** pecūniam postulāvērunt.
..... pecūniam postulāvit.

3 **fīliī** epistulam legēbant.
..... epistulam legēbat.

4 **fēminae** fābulam laudāvērunt.
..... fābulam laudāvit.

5 **lībertī** erant cīvēs.
lībertus erat ......

F Translate each sentence, then change the word in boldface from the singular to the plural, and translate again.

> For example: puerī **servum** vīdērunt.
> *The boys saw the slave.*
> This becomes: puerī **servōs** vīdērunt.
> *The boys saw the slaves.*

1 puerī **leōnem** vīdērunt.
2 dominus **puellam** audīvit.
3 centuriō **amīcum** salūtāvit.
4 agricolae **gladiātōrem** laudāvērunt.
5 cīvēs **servō** pecūniam trādidērunt.
6 coquus **mercātōrī** cēnam parāvit.
7 māter **fīliō** nōn crēdidit.
8 ancillae **fēminae** respondērunt.

G Translate each sentence, then change the word in boldface from the plural to the singular, and translate again.

For example: vēnālīciī **mercātōribus** pecūniam dedērunt.
The slave-dealers gave money to the merchants.
This becomes: vēnālīciī mercātōrī pecūniam dedērunt.
The slave-dealers gave money to the merchant.

1 dominus **servōs** īnspexit.

2 āthlētae **mercātōrēs** vituperāvērunt.

3 vēnālīcius **ancillās** vēndēbat.

4 senex **āctōrēs** spectābat.

5 gladiātōrēs **leōnibus** cibum dedērunt.

6 iuvenēs **puellīs** statuam ostendērunt.

7 cīvēs **āctōribus** favērunt.

8 puer **amīcīs** nōn respondit.

Verbs

A Words like **portō**, **doceō**, **trahō**, **capiō**, and **audiō** are known as **verbs**. They usually indicate an action or a state of affairs.

B In Latin the ending of the verb indicates the **person** who is doing the action. English uses pronoun subjects as follows:

	SINGULAR	PLURAL
1st person	I	we
2nd person	you	you
3rd person	s/he, it	they

C In Unit 1, you have met three tenses of verbs:

PRESENT TENSE	portō	*I carry*
	portās	*you (sing.) carry*
	portat	*s/he carries*
	portāmus	*we carry*
	portātis	*you (pl.) carry*
	portant	*they carry*
IMPERFECT TENSE	portābam	*I was carrying*
	portābās	*you (sing.) were carrying*
	portābat	*s/he was carrying*
	portābāmus	*we were carrying*
	portābātis	*you (pl.) were carrying*
	portābant	*they were carrying*
PERFECT TENSE	portāvī	*I carried*
	portāvistī	*you (sing.) carried*
	portāvit	*s/he carried*
	portāvimus	*we carried*
	portāvistis	*you (pl.) carried*
	portāvērunt	*they carried*

D English has more than one way of translating each of these tenses.

- The present tense indicates an action or state happening now. **portō** can mean *I carry*, *I am carrying*, or *I do carry*.

- The imperfect tense indicates a repeated or incomplete past action or state. **portābam** can mean *I was carrying*, *I did carry*, *I used to carry*, or *I began to carry*.

- The perfect tense indicates a single or complete past action or state. **portāvī** can mean *I carried*, *I have carried*, or *I did carry*.

E Just as nouns have declensions, verbs have families known as **conjugations**, based on the different vowel combinations found in front of the personal endings. The full table of verb endings met in Unit 1 is as follows:

	first conjugation	*second conjugation*	*third conjugation*	*fourth conjugation*
PRESENT TENSE	portō	doceō	trahō	audiō
	portās	docēs	trahis	audīs
	portat	docet	trahit	audit
	portāmus	docēmus	trahimus	audīmus
	portātis	docētis	trahitis	audītis
	portant	docent	trahunt	audiunt
IMPERFECT TENSE	portābam	docēbam	trahēbam	audiēbam
	portābās	docēbās	trahēbās	audiēbās
	portābat	docēbat	trahēbat	audiēbat
	portābāmus	docēbāmus	trahēbāmus	audiēbāmus
	portābātis	docēbātis	trahēbātis	audiēbātis
	portābant	docēbant	trahēbant	audiēbant
PERFECT TENSE	portāvī	docuī	trāxī	audīvī
	portāvistī	docuistī	trāxistī	audīvistī
	portāvit	docuit	trāxit	audīvit
	portāvimus	docuimus	trāximus	audīvimus
	portāvistis	docuistis	trāxistis	audīvistis
	portāvērunt	docuērunt	trāxērunt	audīvērunt

F In section E, find the Latin words for:

1 They were carrying; you (*sing.*) were teaching; she was dragging; I was listening; you (*pl.*) were carrying.

2 He heard; they dragged; I taught; we listened; you (*sing.*) carried.

3 I teach; we drag; she hears; you (*pl.*) drag; they carry.

G Translate these examples of the present tense:

1 ego dormiō; servus dormit; nōs dormīmus; servī dormiunt.

2 servī labōrant; tū labōrās; servus labōrat; ego labōrō.

3 intrant; intrās; intrat; intrō.

4 sedēmus; sedeō; sedent; sedēs.

5 veniō; venīmus; veniunt; venītis.

H Further examples of all three tenses:

1 servī ambulant; servī ambulābant; servī ambulāvērunt.

2 servus labōrat; servus labōrābat; servus labōrāvit.

3 clāmāmus; clāmābāmus; clāmāvimus.

4 dormiunt; dormiēbant; dormīvērunt.

5 parābās; parāvistī; parās.

6 intrābam; intrāvī; intrō.

7 fēcit; faciēbat; facit.

8 dīxistis; dīcitis; dīcēbātis.

9 appārēbant; appārent; appāruērunt.

I A few verbs which do not belong to any of the four conjugations are known as **irregular verbs**. This is the most important one:

	PRESENT TENSE		IMPERFECT TENSE
sum	*I am*	eram	*I was*
es	*you (sing.) are*	erās	*you (sing.) were*
est	*s/he, it is*	erat	*s/he, it was*
sumus	*we are*	erāmus	*we were*
estis	*you (pl.) are*	erātis	*you (pl.) were*
sunt	*they are*	erant	*they were*

J Translate each of the following singular verb forms. Then convert each verb into its equivalent plural form and translate again.

> For example: portāvī   *I carried*
> This becomes: portāvimus *we carried*

1 trahis

2 audīvistī

3 veniēbam

4 es

5 scrīpsit

6 fugiō

7 circumspectābās

8 mīsit

9 tacuī

10 erat

K Translate each of the following plural verb forms. Then convert each verb into its equivalent singular form and translate again.

> For example: portāvimus *we carried*
> This becomes: portāvī   *I carried*

1 intrāmus

2 timēbant

3 cēpistis

4 dormiunt

5 sumus

6 festīnābātis

7 rīdēmus

8 surrēxērunt

9 celebrāvistis

10 erāmus

Ways of Forming the Perfect Tense

A Most verbs in the first, second, and fourth conjugations form their perfect tenses by using a **v** or a **u**:

		PRESENT		PERFECT
First conjugation	portat	*s/he carries*	portā**v**it	*s/he carries*
	salūtat	*s/he greets*	salūtā**v**it	*s/he greeted*
Second conjugation	docet	*s/he teaches*	doc**u**it	*s/he taught*
	terret	*s/he terrifies*	terr**u**it	*s/he terrified*
Fourth conjugation	audit	*s/he hears*	audī**v**it	*s/he heard*
	dormit	*s/he sleeps*	dormī**v**it	*s/he slept*

B But there are many other ways in which verbs, especially in the third conjugation, may form their perfect tense. Note the following patterns:

1 A consonant change, most often to an **s** or an **x**:

PRESENT		PERFECT	
discēdit	*s/he leaves*	disce**ss**it	*s/he left*
mittit	*s/he sends*	mī**s**it	*s/he sent*
trahit	*s/he drags*	trā**x**it	*s/he dragged*
dīcit	*s/he says*	dī**x**it	*s/he said*

(Some English verbs follow the same pattern, e.g. "send – sent", "make – made.")

2 A vowel change:

PRESENT		PERFECT	
facit	*s/he makes*	f**ē**cit	*s/he made*
capit	*s/he takes*	c**ē**pit	*s/he took*

(Some English verbs follow the same pattern, e.g. "take – took", "run – ran.")

3 Adding an extra syllable:

PRESENT		PERFECT	
currit	*s/he runs*	**cu**currit	*s/he ran*
dat	*s/he gives*	**de**dit	*s/he gave*

(Many English verbs add an extra syllable "-ed" at the end, e.g. "add – added", "point – pointed." The Latin verbs add their extra syllable on the front.)

4 Changing the pronunciation (usually by making a short vowel long):

PRESENT		PERFECT	
venit	*s/he comes*	**vē**nit	*s/he came*
fugit	*s/he flees*	**fū**git	*s/he fled*

(Some English verbs follow the same pattern, e.g. "read – read.")

5 No change:

PRESENT		PERFECT	
ostendit	*s/he shows*	ostendit	*s/he showed*
contendit	*s/he hurries*	contendit	*s/he hurried*

(Some English verbs follow the same pattern, e.g. "hit – hit", "put – put.")

Unfortunately, as with English, there are many patterns and many exceptions. Learning the forms as they appear on Checklists and by practice in reading stories and writing exercises is still the best way to master recognition.

C Translate each of the following present tense verb forms. Then convert each verb into its equivalent perfect tense form and translate again.

> For example: portāmus   *we carry*
> This becomes: portāvimus *we carried*

1 laudat

2 venīmus

3 quaeritis

4 faciunt

5 dūcō

6 tacēs

7 prōcēdimus

8 dormit

9 reddō

10 petitis

D Translate each of the following perfect tense verb forms. Then convert each verb into its equivalent present tense form and translate again.

> For example: portāvimus *we carried*
> This becomes: portāmus   *we carry*

1 rogāvī

2 dedimus

3 īnspexit

4 ostendit

5 cucurristis

6 respondimus

7 audīvistī

8 timuī

9 laudāvērunt

10 clāmāvistis

Word Order

A The following word order is very common in Latin:

    Milō discum īnspexit.   *Milo looked at the discus.*
    mercātor togam vēndidit.   *The merchant sold the toga.*
    (nominative–accusative–verb)

B From Stage 7 on, you have learned a slightly different example of the above word order:

    discum īnspexit.   *He looked at the discus.*
    togam vēndidit.   *He sold the toga.*
    amīcum salūtāvit.   *She greeted the friend.*
    theātrum intrāvērunt.   *They entered the theater.*

(There is no nominative; the subject is indicated by the verb ending.)

C The following sentences are similar to those in sections A and B:

1   spectātōrēs Milōnem laudāvērunt.

2   Milōnem laudāvērunt.

3   senex agricolam cōnspexit.

4   statuam fēcī.

5   canēs et servī leōnem necāvērunt.

6   mercātor poētam et vēnālīcium vīdit.

7   poētam vīdimus.

8   āthlētam salūtāvistī.

9   mē salūtāvistis.

10   tē salūtāvērunt.

11   Metella clāmōrem audīvit.

12   clāmōrem audīvit.

D Further examples:

1 Caecilius amīcōs salūtat; amīcōs salūtat.

2 ego frātrem cōnspexī; frātrem salūtāvī.

3 nōs gladiātōrēs spectābāmus; clāmōrem audīvimus.

4 vōs cibum cōnsūmēbātis; vīnum bibēbātis; Grumiōnem laudāvistis.

E From Stage 9 on, you have learned to read longer sentences, involving the dative. The following word order is common in Latin:

vēnālīcius mercātōrī ancillam ostendit.
The slave-dealer showed the slave-girl to the merchant.
(nominative–dative–accusative–verb)

F Further examples:

1 iuvenis Milōnī discum trādidit.

2 Metella fīliō dōnum ēmit.

3 dominus ancillīs signum dedit.

4 nūntiī cīvibus spectāculum nūntiāvērunt.

5 Quīntus mercātōrī et amīcīs togam ostendit.

Longer Sentences with "postquam" and "quod"

A Compare these two sentences:

Pompēiānī gladiātōrēs vīdērunt.
The Pompeians saw the gladiators.

Pompēiānī, postquam amphitheātrum intrāvērunt, gladiātōrēs vīdērunt.
The Pompeians, after they entered the amphitheater, saw the gladiators.

Or, in more natural English:
After the Pompeians entered the amphitheater, they saw the gladiators.

B The next example is similar:

servī umbram timēbant.
The slaves were afraid of the ghost.

servī, quod erant ignāvī, umbram timēbant.
The slaves, because they were cowardly, were afraid of the ghost.

Or:
Because the slaves were cowardly, they were afraid of the ghost.

C **postquam** and **quod** are **conjunctions** introducing subordinate clauses. A **subordinate clause** is one that cannot stand by itself but is dependent on (i.e. subordinate to) the rest of the sentence, which is called the **main clause**.

D Further examples:

1 Metella ad tablīnum festīnāvit.
Metella, postquam ē culīnā discessit, ad tablīnum festīnāvit.

2 amīcī Fēlīcem laudāvērunt.
amīcī, postquam fābulam audīvērunt, Fēlīcem laudāvērunt.

3 tuba sonuit.
postquam Rēgulus signum dedit, tuba sonuit.

4 Caecilius nōn erat sollicitus.
Caecilius nōn erat sollicitus, quod in cubiculō dormiēbat.

5 Nūcerīnī fūgērunt.
Nūcerīnī, quod Pompēiānī erant īrātī, fūgērunt.

6 coquus cēnam optimam parāvit.
coquus, quod erat laetus, cēnam optimam parāvit.

Complete Vocabulary

A Nouns and adjectives are usually listed in their nominative singular form, as follows:

servus   *slave*
magnus   *big, large, great*
ancilla   *slave-girl, slave-woman*
auxilium   *help*

B Third declension nouns, however, are listed with both nominative and accusative singular forms, as follows:

leō: leōnem   *lion*

This kind of entry means that **leō** is the nominative singular form and **leōnem** the accusative singular form of the Latin word for *lion*.

C *Practice examples*

Find the nominative singular of the following words:

novāculam
lupum
sanguinem
parietem
cinerem
stēllae
īnfantēs
mūrō
cīvibus
hospitī

D Verbs are usually listed in the 3rd person singular form of their present and perfect tenses, as follows:

parat: parāvit   *prepares*

This kind of entry indicates that **parat** means *s/he, it prepares* and **parāvit** means *s/he, it prepared* or *has prepared*.

E Sometimes, if the perfect tense looks somewhat different from the present tense, it will be listed separately, as well as with its present tense. For example:

tulit, cēpit.

F *Practice examples*

Find the meaning of the following words, some of which are in the present tense and some in the perfect:

laudat
laudāvit
respondit
respondet
intellēxit
accēpit
salūtāvit
tenet
reddidit
pōnit

G Phrases (e.g. **cōnsilium capit, rem intellēxit,** etc.) are listed under both words of the phrase.

H Some Latin words have more than one possible translation. Always choose the most suitable translation for the sentence you are working on.

cīvēs perterritī urbem petēbant.
The terrified citizens were heading for the city.

iuvenēs īrātī mercātōrem petīvērunt.
The angry young men attacked the merchant.

I All words which are given in the "Vocabulary Checklists" for Stages 1–12 are marked with an asterisk (*) in the following pages.

a

* abest   *is gone, is absent*
*   aberat   *was absent*
* abit: abiit   *goes away*
  accidit: accidit   *happens*
* accipit: accēpit   *accepts, receives*
  accūsat: accūsāvit   *accuses*
  āctor: āctōrem   *actor*
* ad   *to, at*
  addit: addidit   *adds*
* adest   *is here, is present*
  adiuvat: adiūvit   *helps*
  administrat: administrāvit   *manages*
  aedificat: aedificāvit   *builds*
  aedilis: aedilem   *aedile, a Roman political official*
  aeger: aegrum   *sick, ill*
  Aegyptius   *Egyptian*
* agit: ēgit   *does, acts*
*   fābulam agit   *acts in a play*
     grātiās agit   *thanks*
*   negōtium agit   *does business, works*
* agitat: agitāvit   *chases, hunts*
* agnōscit: agnōvit   *recognizes*
* agricola   *farmer*
  alius   *other, another*
  alter: alterum   *the other, the second*
  alumnus   *slave (aquired very young)*
* ambulat: ambulāvit   *walks*
  amīcissimus   *very friendly, a very good friend*
* amīcus   *friend*
* āmittit: āmīsit   *loses*
  amphitheātrum   *amphitheater*
* ancilla   *slave-girl, slave-woman*
  animal   *animal*
  antīquus   *old, ancient*
* ānulus   *ring*
  anxius   *anxious*
  aper: aprum   *boar*
  aperit: aperuit   *opens*
  apodytērium   *changing-room*
  appāret: appāruit   *appears*
  architectus   *builder, architect*
  ardet: arsit   *burns, is on fire*
  arēna   *arena*
  argentāria   *banker's stall*
  argentārius   *banker*
  argūmentum   *proof, evidence*

  artifex: artificem   *artist, craftsman*
  asinus   *ass, donkey*
  āter: ātrum   *black*
  āthlēta   *athlete*
* ātrium   *atrium, reception hall*
  attonitus   *astonished*
  auctor: auctōrem   *creator*
  audācissimē   *very boldly*
* audit: audīvit   *hears, listens to*
  aurae   *air*
  auxilium   *help*
* avārus   *miser*

b

  babae!   *hey!*
  barba   *beard*
  barbarus   *barbarian*
  basilica   *court building*
  benignus   *kind*
  bēstia   *wild animal, beast*
  bēstiārius   *a gladiator who fights animals, beast-fighter*
* bibit: bibit   *drinks*
* bonus   *good*
     melior   *better*
*   optimus   *best, very good*

c

  caelum   *sky*
  caldārium   *hot room*
* callidus   *clever, smart*
  candidātus   *candidate*
  candidus   *dazzling white*
* canis: canem   *dog*
  cantat: cantāvit   *sings*
* capit: cēpit   *takes*
     cōnsilium capit   *has an idea*
  caudex: caudicem   *blockhead, idiot*
  caupō: caupōnem   *innkeeper*
  cautē   *cautiously*
  cavea   *seating area*
  cēlat: cēlāvit   *hides*
* celebrat: celebrāvit   *celebrates*
* celeriter   *quickly*
     quam celerrimē   *as quickly as possible*
* cēna   *dinner*
* cēnat: cēnāvit   *eats dinner, dines*
* centuriō: centuriōnem   *centurion*
  cēpit   *took, has taken*

* cēra   *wax, wax tablet*
cervus   *deer*
Chrīstiānus   *Christian*
* cibus   *food*
* cinis: cinerem   *ash*
* circumspectat: circumspectāvit   *looks around*
* cīvis: cīvem   *citizen*
* clāmat: clāmāvit   *shouts*
* clāmor: clāmōrem   *shout, uproar*
claudit: clausit   *shuts, closes*
clausus   *closed*
cliēns: clientem   *client*
cōgitat: cōgitāvit   *considers*
   rem cōgitat   *considers the problem*
columba   *dove, pigeon*
comitium   *assembly hall*
committit: commīsit   *begins*
commōtus   *moved, affected*
* complet: complēvit   *fills*
compluvium   *compluvium, opening in the roof for air, light, rain*
compōnit: composuit   *arranges*
comprehendit: comprehendit   *arrests*
cōnficit: cōnfēcit   *finishes*
   rem cōnfēcit   *finished the job*
cōnsentit: cōnsēnsit   *agrees*
cōnsilium   *plan, idea*
   cōnsilium capit   *makes a plan, has an idea*
* cōnspicit: cōnspexit   *catches sight of*
* cōnsūmit: cōnsūmpsit   *eats*
* contendit: contendit   *hurries*
contentiō: contentiōnem   *argument*
* contentus   *satisfied*
contrōversia   *debate*
* convenit: convēnit   *gathers, meets*
convincit: convīcit   *convicts, finds guilty*
* coquit: coxit   *cooks*
* coquus   *cook*
cotīdiē   *every day*
* crēdit: crēdidit   *trusts, believes, has faith in* (+ DATIVE)
crīnēs: crīnēs   *hair*
* cubiculum   *bedroom*
cucurrit   *ran, has run*
* culīna   *kitchen*
* cum   *with*
* cupit: cupīvit   *wants*
* cūr?   *why?*

cūrat: cūrāvit   *takes care of*
   nihil cūrō   *I don't care*
* currit: cucurrit   *runs*
* custōdit: custōdīvit   *guards*

d

* dat: dedit   *gives*
   fābulam dat   *puts on a play*
* dē   *down from; about*
dea   *goddess*
dēbet: dēbuit   *owes*
decem   *ten*
dēcidit: dēcidit   *falls down*
dēcipit: dēcēpit   *deceives, tricks*
dedit   *gave, has given*
dēiēcit   *threw down*
deinde   *then*
dēlectat: dēlectāvit   *delights, pleases*
dēlet: dēlēvit   *destroys*
dēliciae   *darling*
dēnārius   *a denarius (a small coin)*
* dēnsus   *thick*
dēpōnit: dēposuit   *puts down, takes off*
dēscendit: dēscendit   *comes down*
dēsertus   *deserted*
dēsistit: dēstitit   *stops*
dēspērat: dēspērāvit   *despairs*
dēstringit: dēstrīnxit   *draws (a sword), pulls out*
deus   *god*
dīcit: dīxit   *says*
dictat: dictāvit   *dictates*
* diēs: diem   *day*
*   diēs nātālis: diem nātālem   *birthday*
difficilis   *difficult*
dīligenter   *carefully*
discēdit: discessit   *departs, leaves*
discit: didicit   *learns*
discus   *discus*
dissentit: dissēnsit   *disagrees, argues*
dīves: dīvitem   *rich*
dīvīsor: dīvīsōrem   *distributor, a man hired to bribe voters*
dīxit   *said*
docet: docuit   *teaches*
doctus   *educated, skillful*
dolet: doluit   *hurts, is in pain*
domina   *lady (of the house), mistress*
* dominus   *master (of the house)*

dōnum   *present, gift*
* dormit: dormīvit   *sleeps*
dubium   *doubt*
* dūcit: dūxit   *leads*
* duo   *two*
duovir: duovirum   *duovir, one of two chief magistrates in Pompeii*

e

* ē, ex   *out of, from*
eam   *her*
ēbrius   *drunk*
* ecce!   *see! look!*
ēdit: ēdidit   *presents*
effugit: effūgit   *escapes*
* ego   *I*
* ēheu!   *alas! oh dear!*
ēligit: ēlēgit   *chooses*
* emit: ēmit   *buys*
* ēmittit: ēmīsit   *throws, sends out*
eōs   *them*
* epistula   *letter*
ērādit: ērāsit   *erases*
* erat   *was*
* est   *is*
ēsurit   *is hungry* (no perfect tense)
* et   *and*
* euge!   *hurrah!*
* eum   *him, it*
ēvanēscit: ēvānuit   *vanishes*
ēvītat: ēvītāvit   *avoids*
ēvolat: ēvolāvit   *flies*
ex   *out of, from*
exanimātus   *unconscious*
excitat: excitāvit   *arouses, wakes up*
* exclāmat: exclāmāvit   *exclaims, shouts*
* exercet: exercuit   *exercises*
* exit: exiit   *goes out*
expedītus   *lightly armed*
explicat: explicāvit   *explains*
* exspectat: exspectāvit   *waits for*
exspīrat: exspīrāvit   *dies*
extrahit: extrāxit   *pulls out*

f

* fābula   *play, story*
fābulam agit   *acts in a play*
fābulam dat   *puts on a play*

* facile   *easily*
* facit: fēcit   *makes, does*
familia   *household*
faucēs   *entrance hall*
fautor: fautōrem   *supporter*
* favet: fāvit   *favors, supports* (+ DATIVE)
fēcit   *made, did*
fēlēs: fēlem   *cat*
fēlīx: fēlīcem   *lucky, happy*
* fēmina   *woman*
* ferōciter   *fiercely*
* ferōx: ferōcem   *fierce, ferocious*
ferōcissimus   *very fierce*
* fert: tulit   *brings, carries*
* festīnat: festīnāvit   *hurries*
fidēlis   *faithful, loyal*
fīlia   *daughter*
* fīlius   *son*
fīnis: fīnem   *end*
* flamma   *flame*
fluit: flūxit   *flows*
fortasse   *perhaps*
* fortis   *brave, strong*
* fortiter   *bravely*
* forum   *forum, business center*
frāctus   *broken*
* frāter: frātrem   *brother*
fremit: fremuit   *roars*
frīgidārium   *cold room (in the baths)*
* frūstrā   *in vain*
* fugit: fūgit   *runs away, flees*
fūmus   *smoke*
fūnambulus   *tightrope walker*
* fundus   *farm*
* fūr: fūrem   *thief*
furcifer!   *scoundrel! crook!*
fūstis: fūstem   *club, stick*

g

garrit: garrīvit   *chatters, gossips*
* gēns: gentem   *family*
gerit: gessit   *wears*
gladiātor: gladiātōrem   *gladiator*
* gladius   *sword*
Graecia   *Greece*
Graeculus   *poor little Greek*
Graecus   *Greek*
grammaticus   *teacher (second level)*
grātiae   *thanks*

grātiās agit *gives thanks*
graviter *seriously*
* gustat: gustāvit *tastes*

h

* habet: habuit *has*
* habitat: habitāvit *lives*
hae *these*
haec *this*
hanc *this*
haurit: hausit *drains, drinks up*
hercle! *by Hercules!*
* heri *yesterday*
hī *these*
* hic *this*
hoc *this*
* hodiē *today*
* homō: hominem *person, man*
* hortus *garden*
* hospes: hospitem *guest*
hūc *here, to this place*
hunc *this*

i

* iacet: iacuit *lies, rests*
* iam *now*
iamprīdem *a long time ago*
* iānua *door*
ībat *was going*
ibi *there*
* igitur *therefore, and so*
* ignāvus *cowardly, lazy*
illam *that*
* ille *that*
imitātor: imitātōrem *imitator*
* imperium *empire*
impetus *attack*
impluvium *pool (for rainwater)*
imprimit: impressit *presses*
* in *in, on; into, onto*
incendium *fire, blaze*
* incidit: incidit *falls*
* incitat: incitāvit *urges on, encourages*
induit: induit *puts on*
* īnfāns: īnfantem *baby, child*
īnfēlīx: īnfēlīcem *unlucky*
* ingēns: ingentem *huge*
* inimīcus *enemy*

* inquit *says, said*
īnsānus *insane, crazy*
īnscrīptiō: īnscrīptiōnem *inscription, notice, writing*
* īnspicit: īnspexit *looks at, inspects, examines*
īnstitor: īnstitōrem *peddler, street-vendor*
īnsula *apartment building*
* intellegit: intellēxit *understands*
rem intellēxit *understood the truth*
* intentē *intently*
interficit: interfēcit *kills*
* intrat: intrāvit *enters*
intrō īte! *go inside!*
intus *inside*
* invenit: invēnit *finds*
* invītat: invītāvit *invites*
* īrātus *angry*
Īsis *Isis, Great Mother goddess of Egypt*
iste *that*
* it: iit *goes*
ita *in this way*
ita vērō *yes*
iter *journey, progress*
* iterum *again*
iubet: iussit *orders*
* iūdex: iūdicem *judge*
Iūlius *Julius (a man's name)*
* iuvenis: iuvenem *young man*

l

* labōrat: labōrāvit *works*
* lacrimat: lacrimāvit *cries, weeps*
laetē *happily*
* laetus *happy*
lambit: lambit *licks*
lapideus *made of stone*
larārium *domestic shrine*
larēs *household gods*
latet: latuit *lies hidden*
Latīnus *Latin*
lātrat: lātrāvit *barks*
latrīna *toilet, bathroom*
* laudat: laudāvit *praises*
lectus *couch*
* legit: lēgit *reads*
* leō: leōnem *lion*
* liber: librum *book*
* līberālis *generous*

līberat: līberāvit   *frees, sets free*
līberī   *children*
līberta   *freedwoman*
lībertās: lībertātem   *freedom*
* lībertus   *freedman, ex-slave*
lingua   *tongue, language*
locus   *place*
longē   *far, a long way*
longus   *long*
lūcet: lūxit   *shines*
lūdī magister   *school teacher (first level)*
lūna   *moon*
lupus   *wolf*

m

magnificē   *splendidly, magnificently*
magnificus   *splendid, magnificent*
* magnus   *big, large, great*
maior   *bigger, larger, greater*
māne   *in the morning*
* manet: mānsit   *remains, stays*
manūmissiō   *setting free (of a slave)*
marītus   *husband*
* māter: mātrem   *mother*
maximus   *very big, very large, very great*
mē   *me*
   mēcum   *with me*
* medius   *middle*
melior   *better*
mendācissimus   *very deceitful*
* mendāx: mendācem   *liar*
* mēnsa   *table*
* mercātor: mercātōrem   *merchant*
* meus   *my, mine*
mihi   *to me*
* minimē!   *no!*
* mīrābilis   *marvelous, strange, wonderful*
miserandus   *pitiful, pathetic*
missiō: missiōnem   *release*
* mittit: mīsit   *sends*
* mōns: montem   *mountain*
moribundus   *almost dead, dying*
moritūrus   *going to die*
mors: mortem   *death*
* mortuus   *dead*
* mox   *soon*
* multus   *much, (in plural) many*
murmillō: murmillōnem   *murmillo, a
   kind of heavily armed gladiator*

* mūrus   *wall*

n

* nārrat: nārrāvit   *tells, relates*
nāsus   *nose*
nauta   *sailor*
* nāvis: nāvem   *ship*
* necat: necāvit   *kills*
* negōtium   *business*
   negōtium agit   *does business*
nēmō: nēminem   *no one, nobody*
Neptūnus   *Neptune, god of the sea*
* nihil   *nothing*
   nihil cūrō   *I don't care*
nimium   *too much*
nisi   *except*
nōbilis   *noble, of noble birth*
nōbīs   *to us*
* nōn   *not*
* nōs   *we, us*
* noster: nostrum   *our*
* nōtus   *well-known, famous*
novācula   *(long) razor*
novus   *new*
nox: noctem   *night*
* nūbēs: nūbem   *cloud*
Nūceria   *Nuceria, a town near Pompeii*
Nūcerīnī   *people of Nuceria*
nūllus   *no*
num?   *surely … not?*
numerat: numerāvit   *counts*
numquam   *never*
* nunc   *now*
* nūntiat: nūntiāvit   *announces*
* nūntius   *messenger*

o

obdormit: obdormīvit   *falls asleep*
obstinātē   *stubbornly*
occupātus   *busy*
* offert: obtulit   *offers*
oleum   *oil*
olfacit: olfēcit   *smells, sniffs*
* ōlim   *once, some time ago*
* omnis   *all*
   opportūnē   *just at the right time*
* optimē   *very well*
* optimus   *very good, excellent, best*
ōrātiō: ōrātiōnem   *speech*

* ostendit: ostendit *shows*
orchestra *area in front of the stage*
ostiārius *doorkeeper*
ōtiōsus *at leisure, with time off, idle*

p

paedagōgus *slave escort (to school)*
* paene *nearly, almost*
palaestra *palaestra, exercise ground*
palla *shawl*
pānis: pānem *bread*
* parat: parāvit *prepares*
parātus *ready*
parce! *mercy!*
parēns: parentem *parent*
pariēs: parietem *wall*
* parvus *small*
pāstor: pāstōrem *shepherd*
* pater: patrem *father*
patrōnus *patron*
* paulīsper *for a short time*
pauper: pauperem *poor*
   pauperrimus *very poor*
pāvō: pāvōnem *peacock*
pavor: pavōrem *panic*
* pāx: pācem *peace*
* pecūnia *money*
* per *through*
percutit: percussit *strikes*
perīculōsus *dangerous*
peristȳlium *peristylium, outdoor courtyard*
perit: periit *dies, perishes*
* perterritus *terrified*
pervenit: pervēnit *reaches, arrives at*
* pēs: pedem *foot, paw*
pessimus *worst, very bad*
* pestis: pestem *pest, rascal*
* petit: petīvit *heads for, attacks, seeks*
philosophus *philosopher*
pictor: pictōrem *painter, artist*
pictūra *painting, picture*
pingit: pīnxit *paints*
piscīna *fishpond*
pistor: pistōrem *baker*
* placet: placuit *it pleases, suits* (+ DATIVE)
* plaudit: plausit *applauds, claps*
plēnus *full*
plūrimus *most*

* pōculum *cup (often for wine)*
* poēta *poet*
pollex: pollicem *thumb*
Pompēiānus *Pompeian*
pōnit: posuit *puts, places*
pōns: pontem *bridge*
* porta *gate*
* portat: portāvit *carries*
porticus *colonnade*
* portus *harbor*
* post *after*
posteā *afterwards*
* postquam *after, when*
postrēmō *finally, lastly*
postrīdiē *(on) the next day*
* postulat: postulāvit *demands*
posuit *placed, put up*
praefectus *prefect, special political officer*
praemium *profit*
pretiōsus *expensive, precious*
* prīmus *first*
probat: probāvit *proves*
   rem probat *proves the case*
probus *honest*
* prōcēdit: prōcessit *advances, proceeds*
* prōmittit: prōmīsit *promises*
* prope *near*
proprius *right, proper*
prōvocat: prōvocāvit *calls out, challenges*
proximus *nearest*
* puella *girl*
* puer: puerum *boy*
pugil: pugilem *boxer*
* pugna *fight*
* pugnat: pugnāvit *fights*
* pulcher: pulchrum *beautiful, handsome*
   pulcherrimus *very beautiful, very handsome*
* pulsat: pulsāvit *hits, knocks on, whacks, punches*
pȳramis: pȳramidem *pyramid*

q

quadrāgintā *forty*
* quaerit: quaesīvit *searches for, looks for*
* quam *than, how*
   quam celerrimē *as quickly as possible*
quantī? *how much?*
quid? *what?*

quiētus *quiet*
quīndecim *fifteen*
quīnquāgintā *fifty*
quīnque *five*
* quis? *who?*
quō? *where, where to?*
* quod *because*
* quoque *also, too*

r

rādit: rāsit *scrapes*
* rapit: rapuit *seizes, grabs*
recitat: recitāvit *recites*
* recumbit: recubuit *lies down, reclines*
recūsat: recūsāvit *refuses*
* reddit: reddidit *gives back*
redit: rediit *goes back, comes back, returns*
* rēs: rem *thing*
   rem cōgitat *considers the problem*
   rem cōnfēcit *finished the job*
   rem intellēxit *understood the truth*
   rem nārrat *tells the story*
   rem probat *proves the case*
respīrat: respīrāvit *recovers, revives*
* respondet: respondit *replies*
rēte *net*
rētiārius *retiarius, gladiator who fought
      with a net*
retinet: retinuit *holds back, keeps*
* revenit: revēnit *comes back, returns*
rhētor: rhētorem *teacher*
* rīdet: rīsit *laughs, smiles*
rīdiculus *ridiculous, silly*
* rogat: rogāvit *asks*
Rōma *Rome*
Rōmānus *Roman*
ruīna *ruin, wreckage*
ruit: ruit *rushes*

s

sacrificium *offering, sacrifice*
* saepe *often*
salit: saluit *leaps, jumps*
salūs: salūtem *safety*
* salūtat: salūtāvit *greets*
salūtātiō *the morning call, reception*
* salvē! *hello!*
* sanguis: sanguinem *blood*

* satis *enough*
scaena *stage, scene*
   scaenae frōns *the stage back wall*
scissus *torn*
scit: scīvit *knows*
* scrībit: scrīpsit *writes*
scrīptor: scrīptōrem *sign-writer*
sculptor: sculptōrem *sculptor*
scurrīlis *obscene, dirty*
sē *himself, herself, themselves*
secat: secuit *cuts*
* secundus *second*
* sed *but*
* sedet: sēdit *sits*
sella *chair*
sēmirutus *half-collapsed*
sēmisomnus *half-asleep*
* semper *always*
* senātor: senātōrem *senator*
* senex: senem *old man*
senior *older*
sēnsim *slowly, gradually*
* sententia *opinion*
* sentit: sēnsit *feels*
serpēns: serpentem *snake*
* servat: servāvit *saves, protects*
* servus *slave*
sibi *to himself, herself, themselves*
* signum *sign, seal, signal*
* silva *woods, forest*
sine *without*
* sollicitus *worried, anxious*
* sōlus *alone, lonely*
sonat: sonuit *sounds*
sonus *sound*
sordidus *dirty*
soror: sorōrem *sister*
* spectāculum *show, spectacle*
* spectat: spectāvit *looks at, watches*
spectātor: spectātōrem *spectator*
spīna *thorn*
splendidus *splendid*
* stat: stetit *stands*
* statim *at once*
statua *statue*
stēlla *star*
stertit: stertuit *snores*
stilus *pen, stick*
stola *(long) dress*
strigilis: strigilem *strigil, scraper*

* stultus *stupid*
suāviter *sweetly*
* subitō *suddenly*
* superat: superāvit *overcomes, overpowers*
superfuit *survived*
* surgit: surrēxit *gets up, rises*
suscipit: suscēpit *undertakes, takes on*
susurrat: susurrāvit *whispers, mumbles*
* suus *his, her, their*
Syrius *Syrian*

t

* taberna *store, shop, inn*
* tablīnum *study*
tabula *(wooden) tablet*
* tacet: tacuit *is silent, is quiet*
* tacitē *quietly, silently*
* tamen *however*
* tandem *at last*
tantum *only*
tē *you (singular)*
tēcum *with you (singular)*
* templum *temple*
tenet: tenuit *holds*
tepidārium *warm room*
* terra *ground, land*
* terret: terruit *frightens*
* tertius *third*
testis: testem *witness*
theātrum *theater*
thermae *baths*
tibi *to you (singular)*
* timet: timuit *is afraid, fears*
timidē *fearfully*
titulus *advertisement, slogan*
* toga *toga*
tondet: totondit *shaves, trims*
tōnsor: tōnsōrem *barber*
* tōtus *whole*
* trādit: trādidit *hands over*
trahit: trāxit *drags*
trānsfīgit: trānsfīxit *pierces*
tremor: tremōrem *trembling, tremor*
tremit: tremuit *trembles, shakes*
* trēs *three*
tribūnal *speakers' platform*
* triclīnium *dining room*
trīgintā *thirty*
trīste *sadly*

trīstis *sad*
* tū *you (singular)*
tuba *trumpet*
tulit *brought, carried*
* tum *then*
* tunica *tunic*
* turba *crowd*
turbulentus *rowdy, disorderly*
tūtus *safe*
* tuus *your, yours*

u

* ubi *where*
ubīque *everywhere*
ululat: ululāvit *howls*
* umbra *ghost, shadow*
* ūnus *one*
* urbs: urbem *city*
* ūtilis *useful*
ūtilissimus *very useful*
* uxor: uxōrem *wife*

v

vāgit: vāgīvit *cries, wails*
* valdē *very much, very*
* valē *good-bye*
valedīcit: valedīxit *says good-bye*
valet: valuit *feels well*
* vehementer *violently, loudly*
vēnābulum *hunting spear*
vēnālīcius *slave-dealer*
vēnātiō: vēnātiōnem *hunt*
vēnātor: vēnātōrem *hunter*
* vēndit: vēndidit *sells*
* venit: vēnit *comes*
* verberat: verberāvit *strikes, beats*
verna *slave (born in the household)*
versipellis: versipellem *werewolf*
versus *verse, line of poetry*
vertit: vertit *turns*
Vesuvius *Vesuvius, mountain near Pompeii*
vexat: vexāvit *annoys*
* via *street*
vibrat: vibrāvit *waves, brandishes*
vīcīnus *neighbor*
victor: victōrem *victor, winner*
* videt: vīdit *sees*
vīgintī *twenty*

vīlicus *overseer, manager*
* vīlla *villa, (large) house*
* vīnum *wine*
* vir: virum *man*
vīsitat: vīsitāvit *visits*
vīta *life*
* vituperat: vituperāvit *finds fault with,*
tells off, curses
vīvit: vīxit *is alive*
vīvus *alive, living*
vōbīs *to you* (plural)
* vocat: vocāvit *calls*
* vōs *you* (plural)
vulnerat: vulnerāvit *wounds, injures*

Index of Cultural Topics

The page references are for illustrations and for the Cultural Background sections at the ends of the Stages.

Holconii   181, 195, 196
Homer   177
Horace   177
hortus   15, 16, 29
houses   11, 13–15, 101, 102
hypocaust   157, 159

ianua   13
impluvium   13, 14
insulae   15
Isis   65, 173, 209, 213, 217
Ixion   120

jewelry   18, 67, 73, 209, 219
Juvenal   83

labrum   153
lararium   14, 16, 207
lares   65, 207
latrina   13
liberta   100
libertus   100
life after death   115–118
Lucian   116
ludi magister   175

make-up   30
manumission   87, 100
Manducus   83
masks   69, 76, 78, 83–84, 86
meals   24, 25, 28, 30–33
mensa   16, 31
mosaics   7, 14, 16, 32–33, 83–85,
    95, 99, 103, 107, 109, 110, 129,
    133, 140, 152, 160, 169, 177,
    223
municipal offices   65
murmillones   135–136

names   10
Nero (emperor)   138, 196
Nola   44

Nuceria   44, 115, 138, 196
Odeon   81
orchestra   81
ostiarius   154

paedagogus   175
painting   9, 14, 16, 24, 25, 32, 35,
    37, 43, 48, 50, 63, 69, 76, 80, 95,
    102, 106, 132, 161, 180, 194,
    201, 205, 217
palaestra   147, 154, 158
palla   30
pantomime   82
Pappus   83
papyrus   175–176, 180
patronus   30, 100
peculium   99
Pedanius Secundus   97
peristylium   15, 29
Plautus   83–84
Pompeii   43, 48, 138, 216–220 (and
    passim)
praefectus   196

Regulus   138, 196
retiarii   126, 136, 140
rhetor   161, 178
riot at Pompeii   138
rooms (names of)   13, 14

salutatio   30
scaena   81
scaenae frons   81
schools   175–178
Seneca   155
Sisyphus   120
slavery   11, 87, 97–100, 134
Sophocles   177
Sorex   81
Stabiae   44
stilus   176, 180
stola   30

Index of Grammatical Topics

Time Chart

Date	Pompeii	Rome and Italy
B.C. c. 3000		
c. 3000–332		
c. 2100		
c. 1750		
c. 1500		
c. 1250		
c. 922		
753		Rome founded (traditional date)
c. 700–600	Greek merchants settle	
c. 530	Etruscans control Pompeii	
509		Kings expelled / Roman Republic begins
c. 525–400		
474	Samnites capture Pompeii	*Duodecim Tabulae*, 450
390		Gauls capture Rome
300–200	Romans defeat Samnites	Rome controls Italy / Wars with Carthage
218		Hannibal crosses the Alps
200–100	Temple of Isis built	Rome expands outside Italy
133–123		Gracchi and agrarian reforms
90–80	Pompeii becomes a Roman colony	Cicero, Roman orator (106–43)
58-49		
44		Julius Caesar assassinated
27		Augustus becomes emperor
70–19		Vergil, author of the *Aeneid*
15	Major public works program	
A.D. 14		Tiberius becomes emperor
41		Claudius becomes emperor
43		
59	Pompeians & Nucerians riot	Nero emperor (54–68)
62–63	Earthquake damages Pompeii	Great Fire at Rome / Christians persecuted
69–79	Amphitheater restored	Vespasian emperor
c. 72		Colosseum begun
79	Last elections, March	Titus becomes emperor
79	Vesuvius erupts, August 24	Tacitus, historian (c. 56–117)
81		Domitian becomes emperor
98–117		Trajan emperor
117		Hadrian becomes emperor
313		Constantine supports toleration of Christianity
330		
c. 385		Bible translated into Latin
410		Alaric the Goth sacks Rome
476		Last Roman Emperor deposed

World History	World Culture	Date
Babylonian/Sumerian Civilizations		B.C. c. 3000
Pharaohs in Egypt		c. 3000–332
Indo-European migrations	Maize cultivation, American SW	c. 2000
Hammurabi's Legal Code	Epic of Gilgamesh	post 2000
Minoan Civilization at its height	Rig-Veda verses (Hinduism) collected	c. 1500
Israelite exodus from Egypt	Development of Hinduism	c. 1450
Israel and Judah split	Phoenician alphabet adapted by Greeks	c. 1000–800
Kush/Meroe Kingdom expands	*Iliad* and *Odyssey*	c. 800
	First Olympic Games	776
Solon, Athenian lawgiver, 594	Buddha	c. 563–483
	Confucius	551–479
Persia invades Egypt and Greece	Golden Age of Greece	500–400
	Death of Socrates	399
Conquests of Alexander the Great		335–323
	Museum founded in Alexandria	290
Great Wall of China built		c. 221
Judas Maccabaeus regains Jerusalem	Feast of Hanukkah inaugurated	165
	Adena Serpent Mound, Ohio	2nd c
		106–43
Julius Caesar in Gaul	Canal locks exist in China	50
	Glass blowing begins in Sidon	post 50
Cleopatra commits suicide		30
Herod rebuilds the Temple, Jerusalem		c. 20
Roman boundary at Danube	Birth of Jesus	c. 4
	Crucifixion of Jesus	A.D. c. 29
	St. Peter in Rome	42–67
	St. Paul's missionary journeys	45–67
Britain becomes a Roman province	Camel introduced into the Sahara	1st c
		64
Sack of Jerusalem and the Temple		70
Roman control extends to Scotland		77–85
	Paper invented in China	c. 100
		79
	Construction at Teotihuacán begins	c. 100
Roman Empire at its greatest extent		98–117
Hadrian's Wall in Britain		122–127
"High Kings" of Ireland		c. 200–1022
Byzantium renamed Constantinople	Golden Age of Guptan Civilization, India	c. 320–540
	Last ancient Olympic Games	393
Mayan Civilization		c. 300–1200
Byzantine Empire expands		518

Date	Pompeii	Rome and Italy
590–604		Gregory the Great, Pope
800–1100		Period of turmoil in Italy
850		Republic of St. Mark, Venice
1066		
1096		
1143–1455		Independent government in Rome
1271–1295		Marco Polo travels to the East
1265–1321		Dante, author of *La Divina Commedia*
c. 1400		Renaissance begins in Italy
1445–1510		Botticelli, painter
1453		
1492		Titian, painter (1489–1576)
1506		Rebuilding of St. Peter's begins
1508		Michelangelo starts Sistine Chapel ceiling
1527		Rome sacked by German and Spanish troops
1530–1796		Spain controls much of Italy
1534		
1594	Fontana rediscovers Pompeii	
1610		Galileo invents the telescope
1620		Bernini, architect and sculptor (1598–1680)
1644–1912		
1682–1725		
1748	Excavations for treasure	
c. 1760		
1776		
1796		Napoleon enters Italy
1813–1901		Verdi, composer
1824		
1848–1861		Mazzini, Garibaldi, Cavour, Italian patriots
1860	Fiorelli excavates systematically	
1861		Victor Emmanuel II, King of a United Italy
1861		
1872		
1896		Marconi invents wireless telegraphy
1914–1918		
1918		
1922–1945		Mussolini controls Italy
1944	Vesuvius erupts again	
1946		Italy a Republic